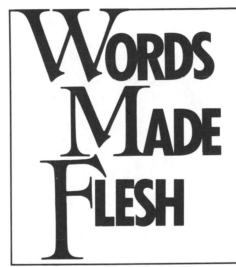

WORDS MADE FLESH

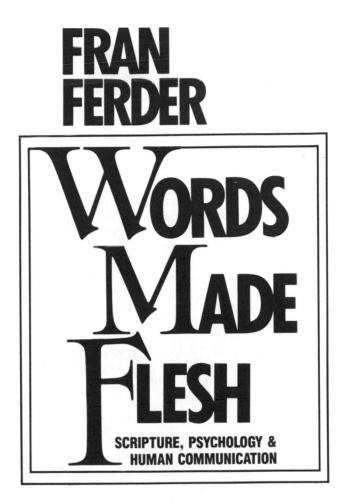

FRAN FERDER

WORDS MADE FLESH

SCRIPTURE, PSYCHOLOGY & HUMAN COMMUNICATION

AVE MARIA PRESS NOTRE DAME, INDIANA 46556

All examples involving the personal lives of people have been developed from real life situations. However, the details, names and circumstances have been altered in the interest of confidentiality. Any resemblance to a known situation or person is coincidental.

Unless otherwise noted, all scripture quotations used in this book are excerpted from THE JERUSALEM BIBLE, copyright © 1966 by Darton, Longman & Todd Ltd. and Doubleday & Company, Inc. Used by permission of the publisher.

All scripture quotations appear exactly according to the copyrighted versions. The author asks the reader to understand that although this material does not use inclusive language, the intent is to speak to all the children of God, men and women.

For Janee Elizabeth Ferder,
my sister and friend

CONTENTS

ACKNOWLEDGMENTS

A book is rarely the work of a single individual. It represents a few ideas of an author, expanded, tested and given life by the people of that author's world. This book is like that. Its inspiration, formulation and finalization have depended upon the talents and support of many people. It is possible to acknowledge the contribution of only a few of them:

The people, many of them FSPAs from my own religious congregation, who have shared their stories with me and have taught me over and over again how possible it is to grow in the ability to communicate more effectively.

Keith Long, a brave little boy whose tragic accident moved me to a deeper understanding of human emotion and its transforming potential.

Archbishop Raymond Hunthausen of Seattle, whose deep faith and consistent willingness to dialogue during times of conflict are a constant reminder to me that compassionate human interaction is an essential part of Christianity.

My FSPA living group, Kathy Graham, Joyce Heil and Pauline Wittry, whose encouragement, affirmation and companionship have provided an environment that is conducive to reflection and wonderfully relaxing and energizing to come home to.

Agnes Schweiger, FSPA, whose constant question after work, "How many pages did you write today?" helped me to stay with the discipline of regular writing.

Rosella Namer, FSPA, who proofread the first draft of the manuscript and gave me many helpful suggestions in the editing stages.

My father, Jacob J. Ferder, whose expert literary skills and patient reading of each finished chapter enabled me to fine-tune many sentences.

My mother, Audrey Ferder, whom I can always count on to affirm my ideas and find my misspelled words.

My family and friends, who listen to me, talk to me, laugh and cry with me, and keep me close to the human.

The many people who have graciously welcomed me to their conferences and retreats, listened to my ideas, challenged me and encouraged me to write.

And finally, John Heagle, priest of the diocese of LaCrosse, loyal friend and companion of many years, who shares my vision and lives the message of this book with his own words made flesh.

INTRODUCTION

Not long ago I was seated between two young adults in a waiting room. Both were deeply engrossed in hardcover books with colorful jackets. After a few minutes the young woman on my right held out her book and asked if I had read it. I do not recall the title, but it had something to do with psychological self-help. She assured me that it was "absolutely fantastic," and that it had changed her life. As she poised herself for what promised to be a chapter-by-chapter account, the young man on my left leaned over and said: "Excuse me, but you wouldn't need that book if you knew the Lord Jesus." With practiced evangelical style, he held up his book about finding Jesus.

For the next 15 minutes, while most of the other people in the area eyed us from behind newspapers and magazines, my lively companions engaged in an interaction that resembled a combination revival meeting and group-therapy session. The young woman described a life of self-pity and poor interpersonal relationships until she "found herself" in a self-awareness weekend. The young man admitted to a background of dishonesty and immorality until he became converted to Jesus at a Saturday night fundamentalist prayer meeting. She was convinced that psychology answered the ultimate questions about life and that "clinging to Jesus is a copout." He was quite certain that the Lord was all one needed in life, and that psychology was a "temptation against complete dependence upon God."

Only a few days after that memorable encounter, I talked with a middle-aged member of a religious community who had been advised to seek professional counseling. Her life history revealed a familiar pattern: poor self-image, consistent mild depression, few friendships, restlessness and dissatisfaction no matter where she lived or worked. While she recognized that she needed to do something, she made it clear that counseling was not what she needed. She had resolved to spend some time at a house of prayer instead because "I feel it would be an insult to God to go into therapy. If God can't help me, nobody can."

This woman, and the two young adults in the waiting room, represent the extremes of two of the most publicized movements of modern day—popular psychology and popular religion. These have traveled from remote laboratories and neighborhood churches into America's living room.

Weekly magazines that once confined their coverage to fashions and recipes now carry feature articles on improving relationships and learning to cope with loneliness. A sports weekly recently departed from its traditional report on athletics and did an entire issue on the personality characteristics of runners, hunters and sports-car racers. Few American homes are without at least one paperback on pop psychology, and few Americans can boast that they have never been to a talk on interpersonal relationships. One can scarcely attend school, go to church, belong to PTA, or be employed without being invited (or required) to attend a presentation on some aspect of personal psychology.

That is not bad. Any contribution that psychology can make to enable people to become more effective in their personal and interpersonal lives is important. But often the articles and programs seem to promise immediate happiness or complete fulfillment via psychological pushups. They sometimes give the impression, however indirectly, that psychology is simply a contemporary name for salvation.

At the other extreme, popular religion has emerged to tell us that psychology cannot help us, but the Lord can—the Lord according to a fundamentalist mentality. Fundamentalism, or popular religion, comes into our homes along the same paths as popular psychology. One can find Jesus paperbacks in the supermarket; watch Praise-the-Lord specials on television morning, noon, and night; dance to the beat of a Jesus song set to rock'n'roll; or dine at a restaurant which caters to Christians. Like popular psychology in its extreme form, popular religion, in its extreme form, seems to promise a life of happiness and prosperity to its followers.

Fundamentalism is on the rise at a time in history when uncertainty looms everywhere. In an age of fluctuating Dow-Jones averages and political and social upheaval, in an era when our ability to make nuclear weapons surpasses our ability to make conversation with our enemies, fundamentalism provides at least one dimension to our lives that is predictable: It gives us answers we can memorize and solutions we can quote. In a world where God often seems remote, a Jesus-Saves T-shirt, or a Trust-the-Lord billboard might serve, for some, as comforting reminders of God's presence.

We need symbols of God's presence. In a country where a large percentage of the population has grown fat and rich by exploiting the poor, the influence of the gospel of Jesus is desperately needed. But when an abundance of Jesus memorabilia and divine name-dropping serve as the primary witnesses to a person's faith, religion has been distorted and commitment is shallow. When leaders of popular religion acquire personal fortunes, show little regard for the poor and the hungry, and advocate an endless military buildup with a kind of "God is on our side" mentality, then some of God's children have been discounted and religion has become disconnected from the gospel.

The extreme forms of popular religion and popular psychology have some things in common—among them, a tendency toward exclusivity. Each claims human fulfillment as its private domain, and each claims not to need the other.

As a clinical psychologist and a Catholic minister, I have felt the tug between religion and psychology. As a psychologist I recognize that human persons yearn for intimacy and that their behavior is profoundly influenced by needs and feelings. As a minister of the gospel, I believe that the search for human intimacy is deeply rooted in the search for the divine, and that hunger for the spiritual is intertwined with all of our other God-given hungers. When we attempt to separate the psychological from the spiritual, when we claim that we can know God without knowing ourselves and others more deeply, or when we pursue our own fulfillment without regard for others, we become trapped at the extreme edges of life. If we view spiritual life as distinct from full humanness, or if we put more hope in psychological gurus than we do in God, then we have done violence to the very thing we seek, our personal wholeness.

Because of the fads and movements of our time, religion and psychology often suffer a separation that is not natural. The struggle to find God and the struggle to find oneself are too often separate struggles. Christianity tells us that they belong together. We do not have to choose between religion and psychology. Therapy and prayer are not distinct alternatives for our problems. Trusting God does not preclude seeing a counselor. We can have both.

The purpose of this book is to reflect on the relationship between the psychological and spiritual dimensions of human communication. Its underlying premise is that genuine faith deepens self-awareness and the capacity for intimacy, and that being a good Christian also means moving toward personal psychological integration.

13

Neither psychology nor scripture are easy topics to write about, much less attempt to integrate. Psychology is still a fairly new field of study. Any science that tries to understand and describe human behavior faces the task of unraveling the changeable, often unpredictable aspects of the human personality, a personality heavily influenced by a myriad of variables that defy easy identification or control.

Scripture study is also a new area, particularly in its present contextual approach. The writer wishing to relate biblical material to human behavior must avoid too literal an application of a text, and must take care not to derive a relationship between biblical examples and contemporary behavior where none exists. At the same time, since we believe that the bible, particularly the Christian scriptures, offers us a way of life, the essential dimensions of that way of life must continually be sought from the scriptures.

Reflecting on the relationship between spirituality and psychology is not an attempt to obliterate some very real differences between them. Psychology is not simply a scientific way of saying the same thing that the bible says in regard to human behavior. The bible cannot be reduced to explainable scientific principles. Nor is the bible a rough draft for what psychology is always trying to develop. Psychology does not derive its starting principles from scripture. The two rest on different premises, develop in distinctive contexts, and offer unique guides for human beings.

The Christian scriptures were written to keep alive the memories of Jesus and to proclaim his teachings. Their particular focus is the life and mission of Jesus. They advocate fidelity to discipleship. They address the way Christians love, and they offer stories derived from the memories of the apostles to give Christians examples of that love.

The science of psychology developed to better understand and explain how people act, grow and relate. Its particular focus is human behavior. It advocates good mental health. It addresses the way people behave, and it offers specific principles derived from research to guide the development of healthy interpersonal relationships.

This book, then, is not an attempt to suggest that scripture and psychology say the same thing in two different ways. What it does attempt to do is recognize that they share some common ground. They both address human interaction. They both advocate caring relationships. They both invite people to enter into a lifelong process of change and personal growth. For these reasons, scripture and psychology have something to say to each other.

Any attempt to allow the good news of the gospel to penetrate and influence our life requires two things of serious Christians: exegesis and faith. First, we must approach the scriptures with the following questions: What is the context and setting of this particular biblical story? Why was it written? For what group of people was the original message intended? What purpose did the sacred author have in mind? How accurate is the translation, or, do these particular words represent a gloss or a later addition, placed there by a scribe or a translator?[1] Another question that has arisen more recently is: To what degree has the patriarchal mentality of the writer's times influenced the story? Once these and other questions have been asked of the text, we can only let go and approach the scriptures in faith, a faith born not out of blind acceptance but out of honest search and prayerful reflection.

In *The Land Remembers*, novelist Ben Logan describes a kind of letting go that has some application to biblical faith: Lyle, the hired hand in the novel, is describing the old-fashioned art of storytelling. When questioned about why details of the stories seem to change and to grow more vivid upon retelling, and about the reasons for the storyteller's departure from the real facts, Lyle thinks a moment and then responds: "Some things are just too important to be left up to the facts."[2]

Perhaps the bible is like that. Dry facts rarely inspire people's lives. Historical details, devoid of local color and personal meaning, lie in countless books gathering dust on library shelves around the world. Like Lyle's stories, Sacred Scripture cannot be reduced to mere historical facts. The writings of the Christians are too important to be regarded as the literal details of an era containing a static message. We must search their stories, keeping this question always before us: What, in these colorful, alive human stories, is inspired by a God who fashioned a kingdom where all people could live as sisters and brothers? Then, in the end, we must bow before that truth in faith—a truth made more brilliant by the flesh and blood stories that surround it.

This is a book for reflection. Hopefully, it will move the reader beyond the uncertainties of behavioral science and past the dialogues of biblical exegetes to the everyday places of life.

1

IN THE BEGINNING

A Biblical Framework for Human Communication

In the beginning God created the heavens and the earth. Now the earth was a formless void, there was darkness over the deep, and God's spirit hovered over the water (Gn 1:1-2).

Emptiness. Darkness. Confusion. It was a world without a welcome, an earth that held no warmth. In their own poetic way the Israelites described the universe as they envisioned it before creation. In the absence of God's breath, they could imagine only a frightening array of darkness and chaos, a trackless wasteland. It was a place of shapeless stars and uncolored skies, a place where human love had not yet felt a heartbeat.

Yet, it held potential. A kind of yearning stirred in the emptiness. The disarray waited for a breath that would waken it to life. To say that God created is to say that light flooded the darkness, that music and beauty broke into the emptiness, that energy swept through the confusion and gave it direction and meaning. The once trackless wasteland pulsed with life. The abyss, the symbol of complete desolation, was transformed into a home for all of God's best ideas.

All of these ideas shared something in common. The fruit tree and the moon, the seas and the great winged birds, the woman and the man—brothers and sisters, sons and daughters of the God who breathed the same life source into each of them. All were connected at a most fundamental level by God's own breath. God the breath-sharer. It is the primordial image the ancient biblical people had of their God.

It is an image as intimate as it is mysterious. The God of the Israelites did not act from a distance, but rather, drew as close to the sleeping universe as possible, as close as breath. The Hebrew word for "breath" is *ruah*. It also means "wind" or "spirit." *Ruah* has connotations of power. It causes life. It is continuous. For the priestly author to say that "God's spirit hovered" was to say that God's very breath reached out to, went into, and continued to sustain all of creation. The breath of God became our breath.

To breathe into another with our own breath is symbolic of sharing our life, of becoming involved in a relationship that is at once energizing and life giving. It is to become irrevocably part of another, inside of, intertwined with all that happens to the other. The image of God's breath entering into creatures is one of profound intimacy. It speaks of a God who seeks to relate, to be close, to share life as it unfolds.

It is often difficult for us, with our modern translations of scripture and our distance from the life and times of the Hebrew people to fully grasp the deep meaning of many of the images found in the Hebrew scriptures. "God's spirit hovered." God's very breath penetrated creatures! How do we understand a God who shares breath? How do we feel the awesome nearness of such a God?

Perhaps the type of breath-sharing that is closest to our own experience is the act of mouth-to-mouth resuscitation. A few months ago, in a tragic accident in a nearby neighborhood, a 7-year-old boy was struck by a motorcycle while riding his bike on a quiet street in front of his home. As he lay on the cement, bruised, bleeding, and without breath, his father ran out and instinctively pressed his mouth to his child's and began to breathe his own breath into his son's lungs. It was an effort to stir to life. It was saving action—the kind of saving action so characteristic of the parent God.

Sometimes at accident scenes and swimming pools one person literally puts his or her breath into another's lungs. At other times the breath that gives life is a word of encouragement, an hour of time, an expression of love. Whenever our words and actions energize one another, we are participating in the ongoing process of creation.

Hover is another word in the lyrical story of beginnings that adds to our imagery of the way God relates. "God's spirit hovered."[3] The word *hover* refers to the characteristic flight pattern of an eagle extant in the biblical world. The eagle hung in the air over its young in a fashion which the ancient people perceived as protective. When it was time for the young eagles to learn to fly, the parent eagle would take one eaglet at a time upon her wings. She soared high above the cliffs, dropped the eaglet, then hovered around it as it struggled to move its wings in first flight. If the eaglet fell too close to the ground without flying, or encountered any danger, the parent would swoop down and catch the faltering baby on her wings.

It was this image of the hovering eagle, ever ready to swoop down to save her young, that spoke to the people of their God. Yahweh was seen as the protective mother, hovering over the dark and confused world, watching, noticing, ready to reach out with saving action. This image appears elsewhere in the writings of the Pentateuch:

> "You yourselves have seen what I did with the Egyptians,
> how I carried you on eagle's wings and brought you to
> myself" (Ex 19:4).

> "Like an eagle watching its nest,
> hovering over its young,
> he spreads out his wings to hold him,
> he supports him on his pinions" (Dt 32:11).

The image is one of a tender, caring God who hovers over all of creation, eager to carry that which cannot yet carry itself.

Our contemporary usage of the word *hover* does not equip us to appreciate its biblical sense. We tend to think of a hovering person as an annoyance, as someone who is overprotective, interfering, bothersome. The biblical term has none of these connotations. The hovering eagle of the Hebrew scriptures is unobtrusively watchful. Her first concern is to teach her young to fly alone in safety. She swoops into their space only if they are endangered and need her. Her hovering is a stance of attentiveness. It is this same unobtrusive watchfulness that describes the God of the Israelites.

God the breath-sharer. Energizing. Attending. Enabling. Seeking to relate. These are some of the same images used to describe healthy interpersonal communication. People who are psychologically healthy are attentive to one another. They enable others to grow or to "fly alone." They behave in ways that energize others. They seek to maintain relationships in their lives.

Breathing. Hovering. When our lives most reflect the sacred pattern that brought us into being, perhaps then we are closest to the holy, and therefore, the most whole.

Creation As God's Spoken Word

There is a final image of God used by the Genesis poet that speaks even more directly about God as communicator: "God said, 'Let there be light' " (Gn 1:3). God said. God spoke a word. God used the vehicle of words, the medium of spoken communication, to effect creation. It was a word that took away the darkness and brought light to the black confusion. It was a word that gathered the great bodies of water and gave them clear boundaries. It was a word that named the sky and colored the earth. It was a word that encouraged birds to fly and invited animals to crawl. It was a word that put life into seeds and flavored the fruits. And in a final burst of most intimate communication, it was a word that called forth the woman and the man and made them images of the divine.

The universe stirred because God noticed the darkness and saw there a potential. Creation groaned into being because it was warmed with breath. Life happened because a word was spoken. God called it good.

To create is to put something of ourselves into our creation. It implies self-revelation, making known our inner being. It is in this sense that we can speak of God wanting to be known, wanting to speak, to say a word about the divine. To know creation is to know something of the taste and smell and sound and feel of God. It is to catch God's word, to hear the voice of the divine.

The poetic Hebrew images provide a framework for reflecting on human communication in a biblical sense: In the beginning, God's spirit hovered over the water. In the beginning, God reached out with a breath of encouragement to all that was bleak and helpless. In the beginning, God became attached to all of creation. In the beginning, God uttered words that gave energy and life. In the beginning, God communicated.

The Call to Human Communication

Our lives today are often not unlike the trackless wasteland of the Genesis world before God's breath. We sometimes seem empty, unsure, without a clear vision or a strong purpose. We stumble against the darkness of broken promises and forgotten dreams. We ache for closeness and fear it at the same time. We yearn for a friend who will stay with us a little longer than the last one, for someone who will know us and find us beautiful. We struggle to say the right words, or enough words, and wonder if anyone has heard. We wrestle with our feelings, unsure of their names and even less sure of their meaning. In our darkness we look for someone to hover over our barren lives and see there a potential for intimacy. We wait for breath. We listen for a word.

Creation is a continuous process. Breathing, hovering and speaking are more than biblical images of idyllic times at the dawn of creation. They are real life experiences needed in all ages. There will always be darkness in human hearts and emptiness in human lives. There will always be confusion in our world. The invitation to participate in and continue the communication process we call creation was extended to all people as part of the entire creative act:

> God said, "Let us make man [and woman] in our own image, in the likeness of ourselves, and let them be masters of the fish of the sea, the birds of heaven, the cattle, all the wild beasts and all the reptiles that crawl upon the earth."

> God created man in the image of himself,
> in the image of God he created him,
> male and female he created them.

> God blessed them, saying to them,
> "Be fruitful, multiply, fill the earth
> and conquer it" (Gn 1:26-28).

For the God of the Israelites, part of the very act of creating was to pass on the creative power. Empowerment is expressed by vivid descriptions of reproduction, growth, and governance: The earth produces vegetation; the waters teem with life; the light governs the day and night; animals and people multiply and fill the earth (Gn 1:11-29). The message is clear: What God did for creatures, creatures must now do for each other. No longer is new life attributed to the direct intervention of a hovering God acting in isolation. From plants to people, life is passed on. God's way of bringing forth new life is to enable creatures to bring it forth among themselves.

As the creation story unfolds, the man and the woman come into prominence. With the animals and plants they share the call to transmit physical life. But their responsibilities go even farther. It is not enough to reproduce. It is not enough to draw nourishment from the earth. For them, there is a greater responsibility. They are to have the blessing and the burden of dominion—care for the earth. They are to be God's special representatives. Co-creators. Breath-sharers.

Like the God in whose likeness they are fashioned, the woman and the man are invited into a stance of attentiveness toward all of creation. They are invited to let their spirits hover over the earth and over one another's lives. They are invited to speak words that take away darkness. Planted deep within their natures is the primordial pattern: breathing; hovering; speaking.

The Fidelity of God's Communication

Throughout the Hebrew scriptures the pattern is woven. These writings can be viewed as a collection of the memories of the Israelites engaged in mutual communication with their God[4]—stories of their ongoing struggle to be attentive, to energize one another, and to speak words true to their hearts. They tell the story of God's faithful communication and of the hovering breath that sustained the men and the women of biblical times.

The communication never stopped. The Hebrews knew their God as consistent. In contrast to the gods of the pagans who could be "on and off" or "hot or cold," Yahweh was steadfastly for the Chosen People. This God was constantly hovering over their lives, forever breathing life into them, always uttering a word that enabled them to continue their journey. The Hebrews heard this continuous communication through the great prophets and teachers of the scriptures.

Through Moses, through Abram, Isaac and Jacob, through Ruth, Judith and Esther, through the judges and kings, through Job, Isaiah and Jeremiah, through the prophets of later years, Yahweh communicated with the people and revealed more and more of the divine.

Sometimes the message was angry; sometimes it was tender. There was pain and there was triumph, correction and encouragement. But, whatever the content of the communication, it always assured the people of Yahweh's continuing presence in their lives. Theirs was not a love-you-then-leave-you God. They did not follow a deity of whims and bargains. God was not a silent monarch who had entered into their lives, but rather, an attentive parent, a sharing friend, an expressive lover. The more God spoke, the more the people experienced a progressive deepening of their relationship with the divine. That is usually what happens when communication occurs consistently over time.

The same God who spoke to the darkness and made a promise to the earth spoke again to Abram:

> Yahweh said to Abram, "Leave your country, your family and your father's house, for the land I will show you. I will make you a great nation; I will bless you and make your name so famous that it will be used as a blessing" (Gn 12:1-2).

A word. An invitation. A promise. It was a word that pulled forward. An invitation to risk. A promise of continued presence. Later there were other words and new invitations. But always the promise was the same: I will stay with you. I will keep communicating. There will always be a word for you.

> There was a famine in the land . . . and Isaac went to Abimelech, the Philistine king at Gerar. Yahweh appeared to him and said, "Do not go down into Egypt; stay in the land I shall tell you of. Remain for the present here in this land, and I will be with you and bless you" (Gn 26:1-3).

> Yahweh said to Jacob, "Go back to the land of your forefathers and to your kindred; and I will be with you" (Gn 31:3-4).

Throughout their history, there were new things for the Israelites to learn about themselves in relationship to their God. Sometimes God spoke regularly. At other times the communication was infrequent. But God never left them.

Through Ruth there was a word on faithfulness. With Esther, a message of courage. In Judith, an expression of inner strength and sense of purpose. Job brought the Israelites to a new understanding of suffering and pain. Jeremiah reminded them that they were as clay in the hands of a potter—needing shaping and firing by Yahweh. Isaiah gave them a new vision and a renewed sense of hope for tomorrow.

Healing words. Grieving words. Challenging words. A word to console. A word to correct. A word to forgive. But always, a word.

A New Beginning and A New Word

There is yet another word to consider, another significant story of beginnings. It was a renewed message from an ever-responsive God, a communication even more personal:

> In the beginning was the Word:
> the Word was with God
> and the Word was God. . . .
>
> The Word was the true light
> that enlightens all men;
> and he was coming into the world. . . .
>
> The Word was made flesh,
> he lived among us,
> and we saw his glory. . . (Jn 1:1,9,14).

The evangelist John saw Jesus as the ultimate communication of God. The notion of divine communication through the person of Jesus was so real to John that he identified him simply as "the Word," the utterance of God. Through Jesus, God communicated even more intimately with people.

Through Jesus, God held children, embraced sinners, wept for the dead. Through Jesus, God met with skeptics and ate with outcasts. Through Jesus, God talked, listened, felt, confronted, cared, touched, self-disclosed—became involved in all of the expressions of personal communication that are associated with intimacy.

Many of Jesus' own words were spoken in an effort to help people better understand the kingdom of God. He talked of it as a kingdom or a reign of love, love defined as attentive service, honest speech, forgiveness, presence. His words were an echo of the Genesis call to breathe life into others. They were reminiscent of an ancient relationship and an earlier intimacy: breathing, hovering, speaking.

Jesus' final words to those who were closest to him summarized this message and contained an urgent invitation to take it more seriously:

> This is my commandment:
> love one another,
> as I have loved you (Jn 15:12).

Love as I have loved. Continue the communication process. Grow as close to one another as I have grown to you.

In the beginning was the breath. It became life for a chaotic world. In the beginning was the word. It became flesh for searching hearts. Today, the chaos and the searching still linger in our world and in our hearts. Sustained still by the breath and by the flesh, Christians are called to breathe life into the chaos and to speak a word of love to the seekers.

They do this by the way they relate. They do it by sharing breath and by enfleshing the Word in their lives. They do it by communicating with one another along the way.

The Biblical Vision Applied to Life

How does the biblical vision of communication relate to life? How does God's way of relating touch our own attempts to relate to one another?

Research in human behavior in the last decade has focused heavily on the kinds of interpersonal skills people need in order to communicate effectively. From a psychological perspective, effective communication is a style of talking and behaving that sustains relationships over time. Certain characteristics are essential in order for communication to be considered effective. They include the ability to:

— recognize and express feelings

— reflect accurately on one's behavior

— listen and be attentive

— care genuinely for others

— self-disclose appropriately

— be at home with oneself

— verbalize thoughts and feelings clearly

— manage conflict effectively

Psychologists suggest that the presence of these characteristics in human interactions enables relationships to be mutual sources of life and energy. When the characteristics are absent, relationships tend to be short term, superficial and conflictive. In such situations people's lives are like the chaotic world of an absent God: confused, empty, dark.

Not long ago, a young woman named Kate told me about a letter she had once received from her father. It contained the following paragraph:

> You have your mother and I very upset. We haven't slept good for weeks and my ulcer has been acting up. Everytime I think about what you are doing I wonder where we went wrong. Going with that divorced man is going to ruin the whole family. Don't you care about us? It's not that we don't like Tom. But Kate, he's not for you. In the eyes of the church he's married. He's probably talked you into believing that it's all OK and that we're just old fashioned. You're always together. You can't tell me that nothing will come of it or that it's all innocent. If you love us, you'll take my advice. This is for your own good. Mother and I love you very much.

A few days after receiving the letter, Kate went home to discuss the situation with her parents. When she told them how angry and hurt she felt about the letter, her father responded: "Everybody's always talking about communication these days. I was just trying to communicate."

Kate's father might have had the best of intentions. He might well have been trying to communicate in the fashion that was familiar to him. But his letter did not feel like communication to Kate. It felt like a cruel attack. The two are different. What went wrong?

Kate's father wrongly assumed that all expressions of thought or feeling constitute communication. He believed, as is common, that saying (or writing) words to another equals communication. That is not the case. Words have to have certain characteristics before they can actually serve a communication function. The letter Kate's father wrote contained a number of statements that actually inhibit effective communication:

> **"You have your mother and I very upset. We haven't slept good for weeks and my ulcer has been acting up."**

This is a *guilt inducer*. Whenever we suggest that another person is responsible for our discomfort, the other person will likely feel manipulated and angry. The hidden meaning in such a statement is "I am suffering because of you, so feel guilty enough to stop doing what you are doing to cause me so much pain."

26

> "Everytime I think about what you are doing I wonder where we went wrong."

This is *martyr behavior*. When we put ourselves down in front of another, we are trying to manipulate the other person into feeling bad enough to accept all of the responsibility for the conflict and, hopefully, change the offending behavior according to our desires.

> "Going with that divorced man is going to ruin the whole family."

This is a rather brutal *attack*. It is a statement of *blame*. It attempts to make another feel responsible for a family's pain, and it is another form of manipulation.

> "Kate, he's not for you. In the eyes of the church he's married."

This is *advice*. Giving advice to another, especially to an adult who has not asked for advice, usually elicits anger and resentment. Kate indicated that she felt about 6 years old when she read this portion of her father's letter.

> "He's probably talked you into believing it's all OK and that we're just old fashioned."

This is an unfair *assumption* and *judgment*. To assume motives of behavior for another person is as dangerous as it is unfair. It clouds real issues and almost always creates a great deal of anger. Judgmental statements usually come from rumination. The person who is upset dwells on the situation, goes over and over the scenario mentally, and then begins to make assumptions involving the assignment of guilt. It is not uncommon for people to actually believe the assumptions they make about others under such circumstances.

> "You're always together. You can't tell me that nothing will come of it, or that it's all innocent."

This is an *accusation* charged with *suspicion*. Such statements are experienced as attacks.

"If you love us, you'll take my advice."

This is a *bribe* and a *test*. Whenever we equate love with obedience we are setting ourselves up for disappointment. Asking for proof of love from another usually puts the relationship on very untrusting grounds.

"Mother and I love you very much."

This is a kind of psychological *undoing*. While the statement may reflect the truth, to add a sentence of love after an entire letter of attack rarely feels loving to the reader. Often such a statement reflects the attempt of the writer (or speaker) to ease his or her guilt (hence "undoing") for the earlier harshness.

Manipulating, blaming, attacking, judging, inducing guilt, being a martyr, giving advice—none of these defines good communication. People often use such behaviors because they have learned them from others, usually from childhood. While these behaviors are often deeply ingrained, they are changeable. People can learn more effective ways of interacting. Kate's father was one such person. Because Kate was unable to resolve the conflict with her parents alone, she asked if they would join her for a series of sessions with a counselor for the purpose of facilitating their communication. Her parents agreed. Some months later the counselor asked Kate's father to rewrite the painful letter that had initiated their conflict. Using the new skills he had learned during the sessions, he penned the following words:

> I have been upset and angry lately, and I need to talk about it with you. It is hard for me to understand your relationship with Tom since he is divorced. He does seem like a fine fellow, and I want you to know that I do like him. However, the thought of my special daughter going out with a man who is still married in the eyes of the church is a hard one for me to swallow. I just wanted you to know that, Kate. I know that you will do what's best. I want very much to understand, so let's keep talking about it. You are an adult and whatever you decide to do I will always love you.

This is communication. It is an honest expression of feeling. There is no blame, no manipulation, no expectation that Kate should live her life according to her father's values. He owns his anger and names his confusion. He states his dilemma and his intentions clearly: "The thought . . . is a hard one for me to swallow. I just wanted you to know that, Kate."

A key purpose of communication is to reveal, to make known what is inside the heart of another. Its purpose is not to try to get the other to change. Kate's father is no longer asking her to change or to conform. He is asking only that they keep talking. He has taken a hard look at his own life and values and decided not to force them on anyone else. He has reached out to his daughter with an honest expression of feeling. He has asked that they keep communication open.

Breathing. Hovering. Speaking.

Communication: Movement Toward Others

Communication means moving toward others rather than away from them. It means speaking and behaving in such a way that a person's life is focused toward relationships. Effective communication is thus that style of interacting that moves people toward friendship and intimacy.

Just as the dark and empty world was pulled toward the light by an attentive, speaking God, so too, the daughters and sons of God move toward each other and into the light with attentive gestures and caring words. They promote or hinder one another's growth along the way by the manner in which they interact.

2

ON THAT DAY
GOD LISTENED

Listening As a Biblical Stance
Toward Creation

At the conclusion of the priestly account of creation, the author says God rested:

> God blessed the seventh day and made it holy, because on
> that day he had rested after all his work of creating (Gn
> 2:3).

The Hebrew *menuha* is translated "rested." In *The Sabbath* Abraham Heschel says that *menuha* actually implies something much more active than the English word *rest*. According to Heschel, *menuha* means "purposeful contemplation." It describes a process whereby one becomes quiet enough inside to see more deeply into life.[5]

In biblical times, *menuha* became equated with the good life—with the absence of strife, the presence of inner tranquility, and the opportunity for reflection. Psalm 23 expresses this notion:

> Beside restful waters [water of menuhot] he leads me (Ps
> 23:2, NAB).

God invites people to move beyond passivity to contemplation. Involvement with God implies involvement with God's creation.

It is this notion of contemplative involvement that characterizes God's own response to creation. Both at the beginning and at the end of the creative act, God is in an attentive stance—first hovering, then contemplating.

31

This closing image of God, absorbed in creation, describes a God who listens. On the first day, God's spirit hovered. On the seventh day, God listened. It is a posture of involvement and another symbol of intimacy. It was an experience familiar and close to the heart of the Israelite people.

Listening to Nature

Ancient peoples were keenly attuned to nature's seasons and events. Their festivals and celebrations often coincided with the change of seasons. The time of planting, the harvest, the dying of the earth—all signaled the action of a power that captured their attention. The Israelites were no different, except that the power that caused the cycles was not a hidden, impersonal force. It was Yahweh, the one God who had created them in the divine image, who had chosen them as a people, and who continued to walk with them. It was Yahweh who brought forth the fruit, who sent the rains to water the earth, who made all things grow. It was their God who changed the seasons, causing the sun to rise and set, and the moon to give light to the night.

Something deep within the heart of these people nudged them to hear beneath the surface of their lives. Something of the listening God in whose image they were made called them to attention.

The earth taught the Israelites to listen. The prophets told them how to listen. The events of their lives reminded them that listening was demanding, that it would not come without cost.

The Hard Work of Listening

In the wilderness the Chosen People listened to their discouragements and fears. They listened to manna and to pillars of fire. As they crossed the Jordan and entered the Promised Land, they listened to their hopes with renewed excitement. They listened to conquests and harvests. They listened to the bitter taste of exile in foreign lands. They listened as they worked and as they wandered. Often, they grew weary of listening. And so they had leaders to remind them and prayers to encourage them:

> "Hidden in the storm, I answered you,
> I tested you at the waters of Meribah.
> Listen, you are my people, let me warn you.
> Israel, if you would only listen to me!" (Ps 81:7-8).

32

> Listen, listen to me. . .
> Pay attention, come to me;
> listen, and your soul will live (Is 55:2-3).

The God who continually spoke to them required a response. The creative word was not spoken in a vacuum. The breath was not blown into the air. The Israelites were to receive the word and take in the breath—and be moved to respond.

The prophet Isaiah understood this response to be profoundly intertwined with the call to serve:

> The Lord Yahweh has given me
> a disciple's tongue.
> So that I may know how to reply to the wearied
> he provides me with speech.
> Each morning he wakes me to hear,
> to listen like a disciple.
> The Lord Yahweh has opened my ear (Is 50:4-5).

For Isaiah, responding flows from listening. The ability to listen comes from Yahweh who has "opened my ear." It is this opened ear, this initial readiness at the start of each new day to hear life, that prepares the followers of Yahweh to have a meaningful word for a wearied world. It is a receptive morning heart that equips us to experience the movements of God and the needs of our brothers and sisters. The prophet saw listening as so important that he identified it as the purpose for waking: "Each morning he wakes me to hear, to listen. . . ."

The Listener From Nazareth

As a Jew, Jesus was familiar with the words of Isaiah. He was schooled in the Hebrew belief that the movements of nature revealed God. His life gives evidence that he too saw the work of Abba and heard the voice of God in the earth, in the people, and in the history of his world.

His attentiveness to nature is revealed by his frequent reference to the earth's symbols. He talked of lilies of the field and birds of the air. He noticed the fields that were ripe for the harvest. He saw beyond the readiness of the wheat to the readiness of human hearts. He used mustard seeds and fig trees to talk of the kingdom of God. He likened the ministry of preaching to the work of sowing seeds in a field. He was familiar with the different types of soil. He sat on hillsides, walked by lakes, and seemed to know a great deal about fishing.

The scriptures present Jesus as a listener from the earliest days of his youth:

> Three days later, they found him in the Temple, sitting among the doctors, listening to them, and asking them questions (Lk 2:46).

The stories about Jesus' infancy and childhood have more theological than historical significance. For Luke, it was important that Jesus be understood as one who, from the beginning, was eager to hear the word of God.

It appears that a deeply rooted attentiveness to that word, as it came to him through his own life experience, was characteristic of Jesus from the start of his public ministry. His ordeal in the wilderness can be seen as an intense listening experience, as an effort to come to a greater awareness of his life mission. All of the synoptic writers place Jesus in the wilderness engaged in a lonely struggle against the attractions that pull at most people at one time or another. In Matthew and Luke, Jesus sees stones—the cold, hard places of life—and wants bread. He wants to be comfortable and full.

He stands at the parapet of the Temple and sees danger. He yearns for protection, for a God who will shield him from life's harshness and take away death. He knows it is possible to seek a safe life isolated from the demands of people and protected from pain.

He looks out over the countryside. He sees power. He imagines a spectacular life, one laden with important responsibilities and filled with opportunities for great leadership. He would be a fair ruler. It could be a good life for all of them.

Jesus could taste the bread and feel the power. He could experience the sensation of complete security—at least for a moment. The story suggests that the temptation to grasp at any one of them was strong. It exhausted him.

The gospel writers were not presenting Jesus as a dramatic artist staging a performance on resisting temptation. His was not a make-believe struggle endured for appearances. Fidelity did not come easily. There, in the wilderness, he fought. He struggled with his life and wrestled with its meaning. He faced all the possibilities and listened intently to the implications of each of them. For a period of time that seemed like forever, he was absorbed in thought, lost in the depths of reflection. Gradually the reflection brought light. Listening became prayer.

Listening for God

It is in the wilderness, in the empty, lonely, unsure places of life, that Jesus hears God's voice:

> *"Man does not live on bread alone*
> *but on every word that comes from the mouth of God"*
> *(Mt 4:4).*

A word. Every word. It was yet another beginning. At the start of his public life there would be a word for Jesus. It would be a word he could live by, stake his very life on. He could give up all the fulfillment, all the security, all the power for the continued word of a faithful God. It would be a word that would be his bread. It would hover over his life and give him breath. He would listen to it in the hills at dawn and in the oppressed crowds in the daytime. He would tell his followers to do the same.

Jesus learned something essential about human communication and its closeness to prayer in the wilderness. He learned that both start with listening. Throughout his public life, he is presented as one who listened.

Listening to People

The story of the 72 disciples coming back to tell Jesus all they had experienced on their first missionary journey gives a good glimpse of Jesus as a listening person:

> The seventy-two came back rejoicing. "Lord," they said,
> "even the devils submit to us when we use your name" (Lk
> 10:17).

Jesus listened to their excitement and heard their joy. He talked with them about the experience. He thanked God for them. He prayed for them. He was a person to whom others could come to share their lives. Whether they were filled with joy or bent in pain they could count on him to listen.

There were the two disciples of John who saw Jesus at a distance and followed him. He listened to their question intently:

"Where do you live?" (Jn 1:39).

He heard more than curiosity about his address in their words. He sensed eagerness in their steps. It was not only the content of their question that became the focus of his attention, it was the whole of their demeanor. He would listen even more:

"Come and see," he replied; so they went and saw where he lived, and stayed with him the rest of that day (Jn 1:39).

Then came frightened Nicodemus—so uneasy about being seen with Jesus that he could only come at night. There, in the dark, he asked his questions and phrased his doubts:

"How can a grown man be born? Can he go back into his mother's womb and be born again?" (Jn 3:4-5).

Jesus spent time with him. He heard his concerns. He talked with him and trusted him. He challenged his limited perceptions and stretched his vision.

One by one they came to him—the blind and the lame, the lepers and the paralytics, destitute people who lived in the tombs and important people who commanded armies. There were Jewish leaders, civil leaders, tax collectors and prostitutes. There were honest seekers and curious bystanders. There were friends and there were enemies. They all came with their needs and their stories to this man whose very presence commanded attention. He listened to all of them. He listened with such intensity that he heard much more than their words. In some he heard their faith as well as their pain. He listened and sent them away, not only physically healed, but with a new sense of inner peace:

Seeing herself discovered, the woman came forward trembling, and falling at his feet explained in front of all the people why she had touched him and how she had been cured at that very moment. "My daughter," he said, "your faith has restored you to health; go in peace" (Lk 8:47-48).

In others, he heard wickedness and manipulation. He heard beyond their obvious words and sensed their deeper intentions:

> Next they sent to him some Pharisees and some Herodians
> to catch him out in what he said. These came and said to
> him, . . . "Is it permissible to pay taxes to Caesar or not?"
> . . . Seeing through their hypocrisy he said to them, "Why
> do you set this trap for me?" (Mk 12:13-15).

Jesus did not sense what was in people's hearts by pressing the "infused knowledge" key on a divine computer. He did not automatically know what people were thinking and feeling just because he was the Son of God. He had learned to listen. He had learned to search eyes and to notice behavior. He had become aware of his own vision and sense of direction. He reflected. He thought. He prayed. He found space for quiet and time for himself. He had developed the kind of personal sensitivity to people that only comes from the hard work of listening.

For Jesus, listening was not easy. The gospel writers tell us that he knew the experiences of heaviness, helplessness and weariness that all listeners know. After days of touring the towns and villages, hearing the pain and seeing the despair, he was saddened:

> And when he saw the crowds he felt sorry for them because they were harassed and dejected, like sheep without
> a shepherd (Mt 9:36).

When he was saying farewell to his friends and followers, listening to their persistent misunderstandings made him discouraged:

> Philip said, "Lord, let us see the Father and then we shall
> be satisfied." "Have I been with you all this time, Philip,"
> said Jesus to him "and you still do not ·know me?" (Jn
> 14:8-9).

At other times, listening surprised him and was a source of encouragement:

> When Jesus heard this he was astonished and said to those
> following him, "I tell you solemnly, nowhere in Israel have
> I found faith like this." . . . And to the centurion Jesus
> said, "Go back, then; you have believed, so let this be
> done for you" (Mt 8:10,13).

There were other days when listening became too much, when weariness overtook him and he longed to get away:

> When Jesus saw the great crowds all about him he gave orders to leave for the other side (Mt 8:18).

> That same day, Jesus left the house and sat by the lake-side, but such crowds gathered round him that he got into a boat and sat there (Mt 13:1-2).

He listened and felt saddened. He listened and became discouraged. He listened and was surprised. Listening brought him insight and self-discovery. It made him grateful and it made him weary. But always, he listened. To wheat fields and to foxholes; to faithful friends like Martha and to less faithful ones like Judas; to outcasts and loved ones; to the festivals and to the Law; to human needs and to signs of the times; to himself and to Abba—he listened.

To Understand With the Heart: In-Depth Listening

Jesus stressed the relationship between listening and understanding, and he spoke of his own sadness when he noticed an absence of listening in those around him. He expressed his concern with the words of the prophet Isaiah:

> *You will listen and listen again, but*
> *not understand. . . .*
> *For the heart of this*
> *nation has grown coarse,*
> *their ears are dull of hearing . . .*
> *for fear they should...hear with their ears,*
> *understand with their heart, and be converted*
> *and be healed by me (Mt 13:15).*

Like the prophets before him, Jesus' seemed to know that listening involves much more than sound drifting through the ears. Listening requires taking in the message and allowing it to influence our life. This in-depth listening prevents the kind of hardness of heart or human coldness that was so loathed by Jesus.

The deep-down hearing that was characteristic of Jesus is what psychologists call *total listening.* It means straining to hear, standing on tiptoe to catch the message.

Our English word *listen* is a derivative of the Anglo-Saxon *hlosnian* which means "to wait in suspense."[6] It gives a strong clue about the true contemporary meaning of listening. To listen is literally "to wait in suspense," to turn toward another with such intense expectation that our whole being is on alert.

Listening demands a conscious choice to expand awareness. At the heart of total listening is a clear decision to sharpen our focus, both toward self and others. It means embarking on a journey past the ears to the heart, beyond hearing to understanding.

Total listening is such an all-consuming process that its presence can never be taken for granted. Many people assume that they are good listeners without ever giving it much thought. They also assume that others listen to them when they talk. Actually, many studies in listening have shown that this is not the case. As much as 75 percent of oral communication is ignored, forgotten or misunderstood.[7] Even rarer is the ability to hear beyond words to understand the deepest meaning of what people say.

Studies at the University of Minnesota have found that people in general do not know how to listen well.[8] Even when people are invited to listen carefully to what another is saying, research indicates that less than half of the message is actually heard. And most of that is forgotten within an eight-hour period. It appears that what was true in Jesus' day is also true in our own: We have ears but we do not hear. We listen, but we do not understand.

Ears That Don't Hear

There are two styles of behavior that are often confused with listening: Pseudo-listening and passivity.

In pseudo-listening, the person attempts to look as though he or she is listening, but in reality, there is little perception of the feelings and reactions of others. The "listener" typically does most of the talking, freely interrupts others to add an important point, controls the topic of conversation, and usually turns the topic to one of self-interest. Such a person does not hear what others say and does not respond appropriately to them for that reason. Common too is the tendency for pseudo-listeners to become bored and disinterested when others are talking. Often they cannot wait to enter the conversation if someone else is talking. They like to hold the floor and seem to need to be in the limelight. Often, because such people perceive themselves as outgoing, they assume they are good listeners. Many times they know the skills of listening, but the information has not moved past intellectual knowledge to their behavior.

Passivity is sometimes confused with shyness. The passive listener is actually not shy, just uninvolved and disinterested. Such a person rarely talks, never takes responsibility for keeping a conversation going, and maintains a posture of distance. Passive people sometimes look as though they are listening, and may even be regarded as good listeners by others. However, the fact that someone does not talk does not necessarily mean that he or she is listening.

We live in a world where there is often more talking than listening—where people have more feelings, thoughts and experiences than others can hear. Our children learn a new game, and no one wants to play. Our teen-agers struggle for identity, and we label them insolent. Men work two jobs, and we say they don't care. Women march for dignity, and we laugh. Old people spend their lives for their families and die alone.

We know the feeling of not being heard. We feel the sting of isolation when we need companionship. We are accustomed to being ignored and misunderstood. And we feel the guilt of knowing that we often fail each other.

It would not be possible or even desirable to expect others to listen to us all of the time. It would not be realistic to wait for the day when all of our interpersonal needs will be met. But it would be possible and it would be realistic to expect that we could learn to listen more effectively than we do.

It is easy for us to get too caught up in our own thoughts to notice another's need. It is easy to become so busy that we haven't time to pause by a tree or notice a tear. Sometimes there is so much noise around us, or within us, that we can't pay attention to what our own lives are saying. In a world where many people start the day with alarm clocks, blow dryers, rush hour traffic and radios, it is often difficult to experience the kind of inner quiet that total listening demands. Often, the noise simply dulls us into oblivion. We are in the wilderness, but unlike Jesus, we are not listening.

Reflection: Readiness for Listening

One of the reasons that true listening is so rare is that too few people have actually concentrated on learning the skills involved. These can be practiced by anyone seriously wanting to improve his or her ability to listen. The skill cluster specific to listening includes attending, following and responding.

Basic to each of these components is the ability to reflect. Reflection describes the process by which we leave the obvious and search for significance. It means putting out into the deep, risking finding something that we didn't know was there. To someone who is guarded, fearful and over-controlled, reflection can be a threatening process. It requires letting go of rigidity and defensiveness. With regard to interpersonal communication, it means taking an honest look at the style of my interactions with people.

Recently a member of a religious community was telling her story of an interpersonal conflict to a group. When someone suggested that more reflection on the situation might help her clarify what had been happening, she replied, "But I *have* been reflecting on it for months, and I don't get anywhere." In describing her "reflections" it was clear that she was ruminating, not reflecting. Confusing the two processes is common and often clouds attempts to understand our interactions.

Rumination means dwelling on something—mentally going over and over the concrete details. It is like being stuck in the mud. No matter how much time we spend reliving the situation in our mind, there is no relief. Reflection, on the other hand, means examining something, looking past the details to their meaning. Reflection usually leads to a clarification of an event or situation. Rumination focuses (or overfocuses) on *what* happened. Reflection focuses on *why* it happened or *how* it happened, and on what role we played in *enabling* it to happen. Rumination goes in circles. Reflection goes forward. Rumination fuels anxiety and depression. Reflection fuels self-awareness. Rumination worries. Reflection listens.

Since reflection is basic to listening, how can we become more reflective? Some people seem able to reach deep levels of reflection in the midst of hustle, bustle, and activity, but for most it is not that easy. Most individuals need some solitude built into their lives in order to reach the degree of inner stillness needed for genuine reflection, particularly in the beginning. Like Jesus, they need to go into the hills. Alone.

Becoming Reflective

The usual place to start is to build some time into each day or each week to be alone in a quiet place. The next step is to become quiet inside, to turn away from the noises of life and wait. Some of the things that help the quieting-down process include:

— consciously stopping all thoughts

— slowing down the breathing and breathing more deeply

— tensing, then releasing the muscles to relax the body

— becoming aware of any parts of the body that seem tight and then slowly loosening them

Once we are relaxed and experience a sense of inner stillness, we are in a position to focus our awareness in a variety of different directions. We can choose to focus on whatever comes into our awareness spontaneously, or we can select something on which to concentrate our reflection.

The process of focusing involves looking at all sides of something or someone. It means fixing our gaze and trying to see more deeply into some dimension of life than we have seen before. We might choose to focus on any one of a variety of areas:

— on a word, a sound, a memory

— on our own feelings or needs

— on the way we have been acting toward someone

— on the feelings or needs of someone close to us

— on world events

— on the plight of the oppressed

— on scripture

— on thunderstorms

— on the first bud of spring

As the process of reflection becomes more familiar, we will find ourselves reflecting often, during many moments of the day.

We might stroll through crackling leaves in the winter and glance up toward the empty tree which shed them. We might gaze at its branches for a moment and then continue walking. We might hear the sound of dried leaves under our feet. We have noticed the exterior of winter, but we have not yet reflected. We have not reflected until the sounds and sights of the season move us to search for meaning in dried leaves and barren branches. When we let the tree speak to us about our loneliness and remind us of the barren places in our lives, we have begun to reflect. When we look back at the tree, standing tall with its gnarled limbs exposed and its summer beauty gone, and see there the cycle of all life, our reflection has achieved depth. When we linger long enough to remember the spring, we have begun to listen.

Self-Reflection

Many people are familiar with the process of reflection as it relates to prayer and meditation. Many are also adept at reflecting on nature, on scripture, and on God's presence in their lives. They are often very good at reflecting on other people and can be quite perceptive when it comes to analyzing someone else's behavior. But some of these same reflective people remain amazingly unaware of themselves and of the impact that their behavior has on others. Often they lack even minimal insight about their own interpersonal styles. Unlike Jesus, they have never gone far enough into their own wilderness to hear their own temptations.

Critical to the whole reflective process, and central to total listening is *self-reflection*. If we never stop to take a close look at our own style of talking, expressing feelings, dealing with conflict, or interacting with others, the chances are great that there is at least some dimension of our behavior that makes it difficult for others to relate to us. In order to ensure that our interpersonal style is helping rather than hindering our relationships, we need to reflect regularly on our own behavior:

— How much do I talk? too much? too little?

— How frequently do I interrupt when others are talking?

— What does my body posture say to people?

— What do my facial expressions say? Am I conscious of what my face is saying when I am with others?

— Do I welcome feedback? How do I react when I get it?

— How do I let others know what my needs are? Am I

dependent? manipulative? possessive? controlling? warm? caring? available?

— How do I act when I am angry? jealous? lonely? insecure? threatened? happy? excited?

— Do I always have to be right? have the last word?

— How do I express my sexuality?

— Are my feelings and my behavior congruent? Does what I feel on the inside match or fit with what I say on the outside?

— Do I experience a real relationship between my Christian values and my treatment of people?

It is impossible to be a good listener for other people if we do not listen to what our own behavior is saying. It is impossible to achieve a deep level of spiritual reflection and prayer if our reflection does not carry over into our relationships. We cannot accurately see the splinter in our neighbor's eye unless we have first seen the plank in our own.

When we become accustomed to noticing life beneath the obvious, when facial expressions do make a difference, when sunsets thrill us, when we look for cues in a tone of voice and read messages in the seasons, when we grow more familiar with the patterns of our own life, then we have entered deeply into the process called total listening.

It is reflection that is the constant companion to that process. Reflection readies us to give every part of our being to listening. It enables us to listen with our eyes and ears, with our nose, our mouth, our sense of touch. It sharpens our perception so that messages from nature, from events, from people, and from our own feelings and behaviors capture our attention and shape appropriate responses. Reflection helps us to achieve that necessary and delicate balance between being self-centered and other-centered. It teaches us when to cross to the other side of the lake to get away, and when to stay and mingle with the crowds.

Attending: The First Stage of Listening

Attending simply means paying close attention—noticing and being sensitive to cues in self, others, and the environment that say something about what is going on. Attending means being in touch. When the word *attend* is translated into Greek, we use the word *diakonos*, the technical term for ministry. In a very real sense to be attentive is to minister. In New Testament times ministry described the specific ways in which the early Christians attended to one another. Noticing the needs of the widow, seeing the plight of the poor, recognizing the sick in their midst—all of these ministry activities are simply ways of describing the early Christians as an attending community. They paid close attention to environmental cues and responded appropriately.

In interpersonal situations attending always starts with *me*. Tuning into our own reactions and knowing what is going on inside of us as we interact is basic to effective listening. If we start to feel defensive and don't realize it, if we begin to get angry and don't pay attention to it, we will very probably react in ways that create distance instead of understanding. Paying attention to our body—noticing if our mouth begins to get dry or if our face starts to feel warm—can signal us to be more aware of our emotional reactions.

Attending also involves being aware of what is going on in others, between others, and in groups. There is an ability that dolphins and porpoises have that bears a striking resemblance to this kind of interpersonal sensitivity. It is called *echolocation*.[9] These animals have acutely developed acoustical sensing. It enables them to immediately tell the physical health as well as the psychic state of one another—simply by being in the same general vicinity. Our effort to attend to one another can bring us close to similar information. It can help us know something of another person's world, to better understand interactions between others, and to sense feeling climates in groups. Having this information makes our attempts to respond that much more grounded in reality, and maximizes our potential of "getting through" to another.

The dolphins, porpoises and whales that have such highly developed communication patterns also have amazingly peaceful interactions. Perhaps our underwater neighbors have something to say to us about the importance of attending with regard to relationships.

Following: The Second Stage of Listening

Both in a biblical and in a psychological sense, following means staying with another. When Jesus asked his initial disciples to "follow me," he was not asking them to step in line and walk in his tracks. He was asking for companionship, the kind of companionship that involved walking alongside him and learning from him. Psychological following involves the same thing: companionship, learning. It means walking

45

along with another and trying to learn something more about his or her perspective. It means doing everything possible to enable the other to reveal his or her world to us.

Interrupting, diverting another with questions, and giving advice, all interfere with following. When we follow someone, we stay out of the way. We do not impose our opinions or press to have our own views heard. We simply stay there, as a companion, as the other person talks. This is another of the skills that is part of the cluster of skills involved in total listening.

Once we have developed an attentive stance, the next task of the effective listener is to help the speaker speak. That is what following accomplishes. It enables the listener to "come and see," to come home with another to see where that person lives on the inside.

Following involves offering "door openers" or non-coercive invitations to talk. We can follow by being genuinely interested, by remaining present and open to the other as he or she talks, and by making brief comments that encourage talking. Following can be as simple as staying with another in silence, offering the other person time to think about what to say, or it can involve offering descriptions of the person's body language: "Your head looks like it's hanging pretty low today" or "You have a smile that goes from ear to ear!" Such statements show interest and indicate a willingness to hear the other's story.

In conversations, both among individuals and groups, following involves doing anything that makes it easier for a person to talk: nodding, smiling, matching the facial expression of the other, maintaining eye contact. Single words of encouragement can also be helpful: "Really!" "Sure!" "Yea!" "Me too!" "Wow!" "And?" "Oh?"

Following behaviors give the message that the other person's story is important and worth telling. Staying with the individual psychologically as well as physically is the goal of following. Looking out the window, reading the paper, knitting, or going in and out of the room hardly encourages the other person to talk.

Following leads us into another's world. It enables us to get a glimpse of the kingdom from another perspective.

Responding: The Third Stage of Listening

Learning to move beyond the obvious, getting beneath the superficial, is the goal of attending. Without the ability to see more than externals, without the willingness to enter another's world, *responding* is difficult and may be inappropriate.

Not long ago I was visiting Jean, a young married woman whose husband of five years had just told her he was involved with another woman and wanted a divorce. Jean's eyes were swollen from a night of crying. Her face was puffy and without the usual makeup. Her voice quivered as she talked. While we were talking, Jean's neighbor, Pat, came to borrow a serving tray. She was preparing for a party. She found the tray, then sat down and began to chat about the hors d'hoeuvres she had made. After nearly half an hour of talk about recipes and party plans, Pat got up to leave. With a flair that seemed foreign to the mood in the room, she made her exit, calling over her shoulder: "Jean, racquet ball is doing wonders for you!"

Pat didn't seem to see the sadness that framed Jean's whole being. She seemed not to notice the agony beneath Jean's polite manner, or to feel the heaviness that hung in the room. Or perhaps she saw, and noticed, and felt, and didn't know how to respond. In either event her behavior left Jean with the characteristic feelings that trail in the wake of superficial comments and insensitive remarks: hurt, angry, lonelier than before.

When our response to another flows from our own needs, or from poor listening skills, our relationships always suffer. Pat *responded* to Jean, but her response was inappropriate because it lacked understanding of Jean's situation. The environmental cues were there, but they were not used in Pat's response. When cues are ignored, responses are almost always off-track. Much human communication fails precisely because people respond to one another without making use of available cues: a tone of voice, a facial expression, a hidden feeling, a body posture, a behavior.

Responding with understanding is that skill which completes the listening process. More than any other communication skill, *appropriate and understanding responding* solidifies trust and promotes long-lasting interpersonal ties. Responding with understanding gives people the feeling that we are with them. When the things we say and do reflect that we have heard their message and received it nonjudgmentally, the foundation for friendship has been laid. There are a number of things that we can do to ensure that our responses to others are both appropriate and understanding:

— make sure that the response flows from reflection

— avoid quick comebacks and snap comments (the old "count to ten" rule is a good one)

— avoid judging and categorizing what others say

— wait to respond until the other has finished talking

— comment on what a speaker has said before introducing a new topic

— avoid monopolizing conversations or engaging in frequent "me" talk

— develop the habit of frequently assessing what other people might be feeling as they talk

— participate in the conversation (remaining silent elevates the tension level in a group)

The Good Feeling of Being Heard

There is nothing in interpersonal interaction quite so energizing as the feeling of being heard, the experience of being understood.

The Samaritan woman of John's gospel had that experience as she interacted with Jesus at the well. After their conversation, she went to the city and told the people: "Come and see a man who has told me everything I ever did" (Jn 4:29). She had met someone who knew her as no one else ever had. She came away feeling that she had been totally understood, and most surprising of all, she felt totally accepted. Not judged. Not reprimanded. Not given advice. Just understood. It gave her energy and enthusiasm for ministry. She began to talk about Jesus and to bring others to know the one whose responses to people flowed from having entered their world.

3

WITH A SIGH THAT CAME STRAIGHT FROM THE HEART

Expressing Feelings In Relationships

At the sight of her tears, and those of the Jews who followed her, Jesus said in great distress, with a sigh that
came straight from the heart, "Where have you put him?"
They said, "Lord, come and see." Jesus wept; and the Jews
said, "See how much he loved him!" (Jn 11:33-36).

Jesus was a man of deep feeling. The authors of the Christian scriptures repeatedly portray him as one who had intense emotional experience and who gave utterance to that experience from the depth of his
being.

Following the death of his friend Lazarus, Jesus is in such a situation. He arrives at the tomb where Lazarus is buried. He meets Mary,
Lazarus' sister, who is overcome with grief. Instantly Jesus is caught up
in the emotional intensity of the situation. Mary's tears stir him to the
depths and move him to experience forcefully the agonizing reality of
the situation. Someone they both love is dead. They will never talk with
him again. They will never laugh with him, never share a meal with
him, never hold him close. He is gone, gone forever.

For a moment Jesus could only do what any of us would do in the
harsh face of death: He groans out a sigh of distress from the very core
of his being. Within moments, the groaning gives way to tears. Jesus

cries. This grown man who speaks with such authority to crowds across the countryside is choked with emotion. This leader and healer, strong in the face of adversity and powerful before his enemies, breaks down and cries in front of everyone. In the face of death, in the presence of his own immediate sense of loss and grief, he allows his overwhelming feeling to be expressed in the most human of ways.

Jesus cried. He cried because it was the only thing to do when agony stirred from within. He cried because Mary was crying and his feeling for her churned in his stomach. He cried because tear ducts were part of his flesh—the flesh he came to embrace—and he would not deny any of it. He cried because he had not learned, or perhaps not believed, that strong men don't cry. He cried because tears were there, streaming from his eyes, and he was too healthy a man to hold them back.

Then, something happens:

> Then Jesus, deeply moved again, came to the tomb. . . .
> Jesus said, "Take away the stone" (Jn 11:38, *RSV*).

First, there is the initial, forceful impact of raw feeling which Jesus does not attempt to blunt or hide. Then there is an outward expression of that feeling through tears. It appears that fully knowing and expressing his feelings enables something else to happen for Jesus. He is "deeply moved again"; there is a second groaning from within, a new churning from the depths that compels expression.

It is as though Jesus, in tune with his center from that initial experience of strong emotion, and relieved by its expression, is now free to move to an even deeper part of himself. Beneath the groaning there is yet another powerful force. Beyond tears something else tugs for release. The groaning and the tears bring him closer to his own heart—a heart that tells him that life is more powerful than death and that crying is not the last response for one who believes. Beyond groaning and crying there is faith.

"Take away the stone." It is a response to having been "deeply moved again," moved past the grief of the moment to the kind of life that lies beyond temporal pain. It is in the context of fully experiencing his own emotional life that Jesus is remembered as transcending immediate feelings. He goes through them, not above them, to life.

Jesus and Human Emotion

The stories about Jesus show that he was able to express his feelings with an unashamed, unembarrassed freedom. The author of Hebrews describes Jesus as having the same human experience that all people have. Part of that experience was the ability to feel and to feel deeply. Jesus experienced the full range of human emotion:

He felt sorry (Lk 7:13)

Moved with pity, Jesus stretched out his hand (Mk 1:41, *NAB*)

"How often I have longed" (Lk 13:34)

And sadness came over him (Mt 26:37)

Then, grieved . . . he looked angrily round (Mk 3:5)

He . . . summoned those he wanted (Mk 3:13)

He was indignant (Mk 10:14)

Filled with joy (Lk 10:21)

He shed tears (Lk 19:41-42)

"I have longed" (Lk 22:15)

"I have loved you" (Jn 15:9)

He was astonished (Mt 8:10)

Jesus was filled with an almost inexpressible zeal to accomplish his mission: "I have come to bring fire to the earth, and how I wish it were blazing already!" (Lk 12:49). One can feel the yearning in those words, the ache moving through every muscle of his body. Jesus knew the pain and disappointment of rejection, the agony of sadness. He experienced the kind of intense longing that pulls at the heart and gnaws in the stomach. At times it moved him to tears, wet and salty expressions of feeling. He churned with anger, struggled with impatience, and cherished times of joy and excitement. His pulse quickened with compassion, and his face mellowed in tenderness. He knew love.

It was not an emotionally frozen Messiah who gathered together a small band of followers and called them friends. It was not a sterile God keeping a proper distance who wandered over the Galilean countryside with women and men together. It was not an over-controlled Redeemer who begged for companionship and perspired in agony during his last hours. Jesus did not feel for effect. He felt because feeling is human, and being fully human is not incompatible with being divine.

The followers of Jesus are to model their lives after his. They are to be like him. They are called by baptism and challenged by his life to be women and men of deep feeling.

Feeling Our Way to God

It is not uncommon today to meet individuals who try, as "good Christians," to transcend their feelings and emotions too quickly. They experience an initial flood of anger or sadness and immediately attempt to dull its intensity. Sometimes this is attempted through prayer. The anxious Christian experiences an emotion judged to be unacceptable and rushes to "give it to God" or "offer it up."

The attempt to overspiritualize the emotional life leads eventually to deeply buried grief, resentments, angers, sexual desires, fears, attractions, and a full range of locked-in feeling experiences. Sometimes, offering up an uncomfortable feeling is not prayer at all, but a religious name for psychological repression. We cannot offer up what we have not fully claimed as our own. We cannot give to God what we have not fully received ourselves. Like Jesus at the tomb of Lazarus, we cannot be deeply moved to transcendent life until we have been deeply moved by present reality. We do not move to the transcendent by skipping over the human, but rather, by knowing it to the full. We will not know the joy of resurrection until we have groaned over death.

As Christians we must be moved with compassion and filled with tenderness. We must churn with anger, struggle with impatience, and cherish joy. We must yearn and want, ache and cry. We must know love.

We may not turn the God-man who entered into human feeling into a stoic savior. We cannot minimize the stories of his emotional expressiveness in order to provide ourselves with an excuse for our own emotional flight.

Feeling Expression and Mental Health

The gospel emphasis on feelings is paralleled by a similar emphasis from the behavioral sciences. The ability to know and express feelings appropriately is an indication of mental health. The inability to do so suggests a lack of full human development and may even indicate a serious mental disorder.

Many cultural, social and religious forces of the past have not always been helpful in enabling people to learn to express their feelings. In a society which has stressed that women are more emotional than men, it has been difficult for many men to allow themselves freedom to express their feelings. With macho images looming before them, they have often blotted out their own tender stirrings and forgotten gentle words. It is not uncommon for males in our society to express more emotion in front of the NFL game on television than in front of their wives as they try to find words for love.

Men have been encouraged to be in tight control of their feelings and reminded not to cry. To the degree that they have internalized these messages, they have been stripped of some of their humanness. They have lost some of their richest resources for intimacy.

Society in the past has allowed women to be emotional but has not often encouraged the verbal expression of emotion. The two are different. One can be emotional by crying, by pouting, by nagging, by slamming cupboard doors. But that does not mean that feelings have been adequately or effectively addressed.

In order to express feelings in a manner that promotes relationships and deepens intimacy, they must be owned—acknowledged to ourselves—and then clarified verbally for others. It is this process that takes away the darkness of confusion in relationships.

Expressing Feelings: The Influence of Christianity

With Jesus as a model, it would seem that expressing feelings and being comfortable with emotional experience should come more easily for those who follow the gospels. However, this does not appear to be the case. In fact, for many Christians the exact opposite is true.

Over the centuries the church was profoundly influenced by secular philosophies of the day: Greek dualism, gnosticism, stoicism, the Puritan ethic. In a world which said that all forms of pleasure were evil, it was difficult to remember that Jesus had come eating and drinking, that he had welcomed the woman who kissed his feet, that he had touched and caressed and loved. Amid those who stressed control, it was difficult to keep alive the memory of the man who had wept over Jerusalem and tipped over tables in the Temple. In a world which came more and more to regard emotions as private, it seemed only natural to let the images of the groaning, sighing, expressive Jesus fade into the background.

During the early fifth century Saint Augustine taught that sexual desire and the potential to experience genital pleasure were not actually intended by God, but were rather an unfortunate result of the fall of Adam and Eve.[10] With the advent of the church's regulations and directives surrounding sexual behavior, and with the pronouncement of anger as one of the seven capital sins, the stage for Christians to be suspect of their feelings was set. It then became easy to regard feelings and emotions as distant from God and opposed to the Spirit. In the minds of many Catholic Christians, repressing feelings and emotions was elevated to the status of a virtue.

It also became easy to divide feelings into the "good" ones and the "bad" ones. Sexual feelings and angry feelings were often seen as bad or at least not very worthy, while the more comfortable feelings, such as joy and peacefulness, were viewed as good. As a result, many people learned to evade their less comfortable feelings. Denying anger, ignoring jealousy, running from loneliness, and turning off sexual feelings became an established way of life for many.

Persistent evasion is habit forming. It does not take long for the tendency to evade feelings to become a well entrenched personality characteristic.

The Body's Response

While a feeling might be put out of a person's mind, it cannot be put out of the body. The energy from the hidden feeling remains trapped in the stomach, the chest, the neck. We can try to dull it with aspirin or drown it with Maalox, but the energy and chemical correlates of trapped emotional reactions stay alive and scream for release. Sooner or later uncomfortable feelings are exchanged for uncomfortable symptoms as the victims of repressed feelings become plagued with a variety of emotionally related physical problems and diseases.

As behavioral science began recognizing the relationship between poorly handled feelings and many physical symptoms and diseases, and as theologians began viewing the humanity of Jesus in a new light, there has been a renewed emphasis in both society and in Christianity on the importance of being in touch with and giving appropriate expression to feelings.

Yearning for Closeness

As a result, many people now find themselves in the position of hearing about the importance of feelings, but find it awkward to express them in their relationships. They have the desire to be more open but lack the tools. They have not learned to be at home with their feelings, to name them, or to express them aloud to anyone.

As a therapist and minister, many of the concerns that people bring to me are related to the inability to express feelings: A young woman doesn't know if her husband is still attracted to her after five years of marriage. A man is confused about the meaning of his wife's frequent periods of hostile silence. A member of a religious community can't understand why her closest friend left without telling her why or saying goodbye. The members of a parish staff never know where they stand with the pastor. A college student can't talk to her parents. A woman is depressed. A man drinks too much.

Their stories—our stories—are told every day in counseling centers and parish offices. They are spilled out over the telephone and whispered in coffee shops. They are sad stories because they tell of the people who ache for human closeness, who yearn for a way to find each other, yet who bear the burden of a religious and cultural heritage that didn't equip them with one of the basic skills for intimacy—an ability to express feelings.

They are painful stories of a husband who thinks it's unnecessary to tell his wife how special she is and how much he needs her; of a wife who doesn't know how to tell her husband about her rage; of a young woman in a religious congregation who cannot bring herself to stand face to face and say goodbye; of a pastor who has spent years keeping his distance and doesn't realize it; of parents who never learned the names of their feelings; of an angry woman and a frightened man who will tell their pain to no one.

There is a paradox to the stories. At the same time that they are stories of sadness, they are also stories of joy. Joy, because they tell of people, many people, who are attempting to break out of the silence of unspoken feelings and unshared dreams, people who recognize that their feelings are important and it is time to give them a name and a home.

Assisting people with this process is an essential dimension of ministry today. Feelings and emotions are not simply psychological realities that Christians must put up with as a result of being in the world. An-

ger and elation are not mere categories of behavioral science that have
no significance in the realm of the spirit. Goose bumps and sweaty
palms are not just inevitable bodily reactions triggered by hormones.
Sexual arousal and pelvic pleasure are not shameful signs of weak self-
control rendered legal by a marriage certificate. All of them—our full
range of feelings and emotions, their variety of physical manifestation,
and their ability to give us pleasure as well as pain—are created by God.
As such, they are all potential sources of divine revelation, God bursting
unexpectedly into our lives with a message not to be ignored.

Feelings: The Work of God's Hand

Most of us are familiar with the often quoted image of the potter
and the clay of the Hebrew scriptures:

> We the clay, you the potter,
> we are all the work of your hand (Is 64:8).

We associate this image with creation. God is the potter. We are the
clay. A potter is one who makes pots. While many of us appreciate the
beauty and art of hand-thrown pottery, few of us have a regular opportunity to watch a potter at the wheel, working and reworking the clay,
smoothing out imperfections, fully absorbed in the task of shaping a single pot. It might be easier for us, with our computer-age mentality, to
visualize a modern factory turning out technologically perfect pots by
the hundreds.

Yet an accurate image of the Hebrew potter, *yatsar*, portrayed in
the scriptures is essential to appreciating the purposeful creation of all
dimensions of our humanness. *Yatsar* does mean to make pots. But it
means to make pots in a particular kind of way. It does not refer to routine assembly-line production. The Hebrew *yatsar* was an artist. *Yatsar*
means "to fashion," "to shape," "to knit," "to form." It implies a posture
of involvement on the part of the potter. It takes time. It demands great
skill. It requires a sense of purpose and a vision. *Yatsar* means to become
completely involved in molding a pot. The potter studies the clay, feels
it, assesses its moisture content, its weight, notices any roughness, sees a
potential for beauty and usefulness. As the clay is molded, first into a
general form and then, much more gradually, into its final shape, the
potter directs its destiny. The potter is involved with the clay, intent
upon it, studying it, touching it, ever ready to make a subtle finger

movement or to press it together and start over. The potter, like any artist, puts something of himself or herself into each pot. In this sense, the pot images the potter.

While the creation of a pot has a degree of uncertainty about final dimensions and contours, it is not put into the fire for completion until it conforms to the potter's vision. It must please the potter. The *yatsar* then is not a hapless worker of clay who turns out pots and hopes that some will be serviceable. He or she is a visionary with a dream, a creator with a plan and an ability to mold dreams and plans into purposeful reality.

The Hebrew authors saw a similarity between Yahweh and the potter. They envisioned their God as the *yatsar* who fashioned them as had the potter with clay. Yahweh was the divine artist, intent upon them, studying them, touching them, molding them, plunging them into the fire, enabling them to conform to the divine dream. This image of God as the potter was used for the people as a nation as well as for individuals. Yahweh was at once the potter acting on all of Israel, and the potter who knit each of them individually in the womb:

> Then this word of Yahweh was addressed to me, "House of
> Israel, can not I do to you what this potter does? . . . .
> Yes, as the clay is in the potter's hand, so you are in mine,
> House of Israel" (Jer 18:5-6).

> Thus says Yahweh who made [*yatsar*] you,
> who formed [*yatsar*] you from the womb, who is your
> help (Is 44:2).

It is easy to give quick intellectual assent to a reference to God as potter, fashioning a child in the womb or forming a people. It is more difficult to spend time with that image, to push it to specifics, to draw implications from it for our humanity.

If we believe that God fashioned us, much as would a potter, with careful purpose, clear intention, full absorption in the creational task, then God must have fashioned all parts of us, our feelings and emotions as well as our arms and our legs.

Try, for a moment, to imagine a shapeless lump of clay, destined to be formed into a human emotion. God, the potter, studies the clay, looks deeply into it, sees there a potential. Carefully, purposefully, reverently, God molds the lifeless mass into the emotion we call anger. Fashioned into the anger is fire and energy. When touched or triggered, it has the amazing capacity to protect, to produce action, to clarify the environment, to compel communication. God stands back and calls it good. The emotion of anger is now ready. It fits the divine plan. It fulfills the creative vision. It is placed within a larger lump of yet unfinished clay and the work continues. The potter is pleased.

If we can regard God as the potter, shaping clay into humanity, then we can also regard God as the potter who shapes human excitement, fear, attraction, jealousy, longing, sexual arousal, loneliness, happiness, sadness—all of those moving, flooding experiences that we identify as emotions and feelings.

God is not a slipshod potter who didn't notice that feelings were creeping into humanity at the dawn of creation. God is not a cruel jester who flooded us with deep and wondrous feelings, but intended that we not use them. God is not a disciplinarian who gave us feelings so we might practice self-control and denial en route to perfection.

Ours is a God of tenderness who would never leave us orphans. Ours is a God of surprises who provides food in the wilderness and parts waters before us. Ours is a God of anger, repulsed by wicked deeds and selfish ways. Ours is a sexual God who created male and female with powerful desires for each other. Ours is a forgiving God who seals our crimes in a bag and never calls our sin to mind. Ours is a God of exciting dreams, of weary journeys, of stirring reunions and tearful deaths. Ours is a God of love who sent Jesus to remind us of that love and to show us that feeling is part of loving.

The Potter's Plan for Emotions

What exactly did God have in mind in fashioning human emotion? Often we discover something about God's purposes by looking more intently at creation, in this instance, at emotions themselves. It is here that psychology and the behavioral sciences can be helpful.

Many psychologists believe that the ultimate purpose of human emotion is survival. Psychologist Robert Plutchik has identified eight primary emotions, to which are linked all other feelings and emotions.[11] They are:

— joy
— acceptance
— fear

58

— surprise

— sadness

— disgust

— anger

— anticipation

Each evokes a protective behavior that enables the survival of the individual as well as the race. *Joy* initiates reproductive behaviors and thus allows the race to perpetuate itself. *Acceptance* leads to incorporation and social interaction, enabling individuals to receive adequate nurturance and care. *Fear* protects by compelling retreat from threatened harm. *Surprise* encourages adequate reorientation to changes in the environment. *Sadness* facilitates reintegration in the face of loss by attracting sources of help. *Disgust* brings about behaviors that force the rejection of something harmful. *Anger* evokes actions designed to eliminate barriers to the satisfaction of important needs. It also enables the clarification of needs. *Anticipation,* finally, elicits exploration, urging preparation for future challenges and change.

When the eight primary emotions are blended with each other, according to Plutchik, mixed emotions occur. For example, when joy and acceptance are blended, love develops; if acceptance is blended to fear, submission results. The following diagrams illustrate the primary and mixed emotions and can be helpful in clarifying emotional experience.

MAPPING EMOTIONAL INTENSITIES

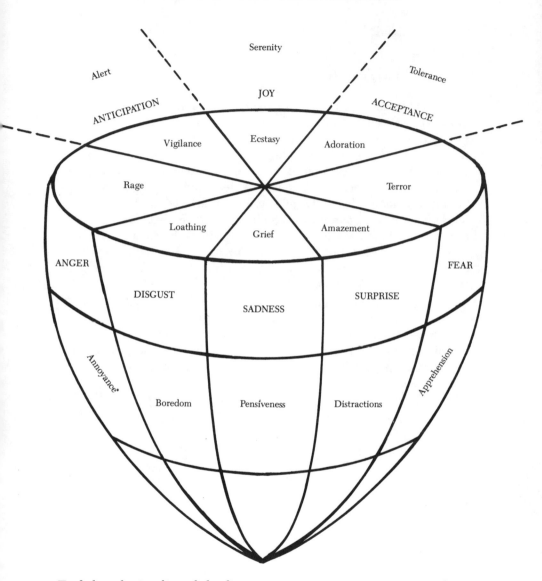

Each lengthwise slice of the figure represents a primary emotion, from its most intense to its mildest expression. (For example, grief is a more intense experience of sadness; pensiveness is a less intense experience of sadness.)

PRIMARY AND MIXED EMOTIONS

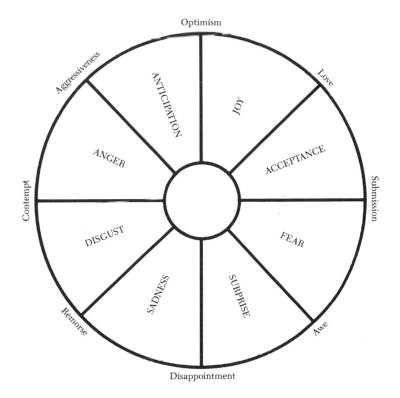

The mixed emotions appear outside the circle between the two primary emotions being mixed. (For example, remorse is a mixture of disgust and sadness.)

More Than Physical Survival

Emotions seem to play an important role in relational as well as physical survival. We know that individuals who ignore their emotions, or who are out of touch with their feelings, do not survive well in their interpersonal lives. In the primitive world failure to notice emotions could signal certain physical death. Today we usually have enough other resources to protect our physical bodies even if we neglect our emotional cues. It is rather our relationships that suffer, and sometimes die, when our emotional reactions are neglected.

When we are unaware of our deepest feelings, we can behave in destructive ways without realizing it. Sarcasm can result from unnoticed anger. Gossip can flow from unrecognized jealousy. Manipulation can occur if we are insecure and don't know it. Such behaviors usually happen because we have not been aware of strong feelings and have acted on impulse. Few people, for example, sit down, think about their inner reactions, identify the presence of jealousy, and then make a clear decision to gossip about the person in response to it.

Ideas, thoughts, beliefs, values, attitudes and actions are all profoundly influenced by feelings. To the degree that we are aware of our feelings, our behavior can be chosen. To the degree that we are not aware of them, our behavior is apt to be random. Random or impulsive behavior is incompatible with stable and mutually satisfying relationships.

Increasing awareness of our feelings, and choosing appropriate responses to them, involves a process that can be learned. That process has four basic components:

— Noticing

— Owning

— Naming

— Responding

Noticing Feelings

People who are in touch with their feelings are in touch with their bodies. They can sense, almost instantly, a slight quickening of their heartbeat, a mild muscular tightening, or sudden warming of skin temperature—and they know it means something.

All emotions have physiological correlates. Emotions are defined, in part, as bodily reactions. This means that certain physical signs can be used as clues to alert us to the fact that an emotional reaction is occurring: a dry mouth, facial warming (and reddening), stomach "butterflies," shaking, sweating, a lump in the throat, shortness of breath. For individuals who pay little attention to their feelings, learning to recognize the body states that accompany feelings can be a helpful first step toward becoming more aware of them. (A more specific discussion on anger in the next chapter will take an in-depth look at the physiology of emotions.)

In order to grow more accustomed to noticing our feeling states, it can be helpful to stop periodically throughout the day and reflect on our bodily reactions: What part of my body does my attention go to immediately? Does any part of my body feel tight? weak? different? Is any part trying to speak to me or get my attention? how? why?

Consciously focusing attention on our body during interpersonal encounters or during times of stress can also facilitate the process of noticing feelings. For example, if I am talking to someone and I notice that my mouth is starting to get dry, I can focus on that for a moment and reflect on what it means. My dry mouth indicates that my emotional state is changing. I am reacting to something. What is it?

This process of noticing the signs of emotions in my body takes much longer to describe than it does to do. To the person who has developed a habit of tuning in to feelings as they are occurring, it can take only a second. To the person who is less familiar with the process, it will take longer, and like any new behavior, may seem a bit contrived at first. However, with practice, attending to physiological signs of feelings will become almost automatic. Naming them, then, is the next step.

Naming Feelings

To the Hebrews, naming a person or a thing had great significance. Naming something meant establishing a relationship with that which was named. Once named, the person or thing could not be discarded; it was owned.

Our own cultural experience may not be exactly the same in the sense that naming and owning tend to be different processes. However, from a psychological perspective naming does suggest relatedness. Giving a name to our emotional experience is an important step in the whole process of coming to be at home with it. When we name a feeling, we acknowledge that it exists. We begin to relate to it.

Giving accurate labels to experiences as subjective and nebulous as human feelings is often more difficult than it sounds. One problem is that many people lack more than a rudimentary feeling vocabulary. Another is that even behavioral scientists sometimes disagree about the exact meaning of many emotional words.

What is important interpersonally is not the scientific accuracy of a name, but its significance for the individual doing the naming. If the name I give to an introspective experience clarifies the experience for me, and if it enables others to become more a part of my world, then it has been rightly named. The following list of emotional terms may serve that naming process.

ACCEPTING[12]
Agreeable
Serene
Cheerful
Receptive
Calm
Patient
Obliging
Affectionate
Obedient
Timid
Scared
Panicky

AFRAID
Shy
Submissive
Bashful
Embarrassed
Terrified
Pensive
Cautious
Anxious
Helpless
Apprehensive
Self-conscious
Ashamed
Humiliated
Forlorn
Nervous
Lonely
Apathetic
Meek
Guilty

SAD
Sorrowful

Empty
Remorseful
Hopeless
Depressed
Worried
Disinterested
Grief-stricken
Unhappy
Gloomy
Despairing
Watchful
Hesitant
Indecisive
Rejected
Bored
Disappointed
Vacillating
Discouraged
Puzzled
Uncertain
Bewildered
Confused
Perplexed
Ambivalent

SURPRISED
Astonished
Amazed
Awed
Envious

DISGUSTED
Unsympathetic
Unreceptive
Indignant
Disagreeable
Resentful

Revolted
Displeased
Suspicious
Dissatisfied
Contrary
Jealous
Intolerant
Distrustful
Vengeful
Bitter
Unfriendly
Stubborn
Uncooperative
Contemptuous
Loathful
Critical
Annoyed
Irritated

ANGRY
Antagonistic
Furious
Hostile
Outraged
Scornful
Unaffectionate
Quarrelsome
Impatient
Grouchy
Defiant
Aggressive
Sarcastic
Rebellious
Exasperated
Disobedient
Demanding

Possessive	Playful	Attentive
Greedy	Adventurous	**JOYFUL**
Wondering	Ecstatic	Happy
Impulsive	Sociable	Self-controlled
ANTICIPATORY	Hopeful	Satisfied
Boastful	Gleeful	Pleased
Expectant	Elated	Generous
Daring	Eager	Ready
Curious	Enthusiastic	Sympathetic
Reckless	Interested	Content
Proud	Delighted	Cooperative
Inquisitive	Amused	Trusting
		Tolerant

If we are feeling vaguely uncomfortable and we reflect on that discomfort, locate it in our body, and give the discomfort a name, we have begun to take charge of it. It will not control us because it is no longer a cloudy force operating outside our awareness. Perhaps we might name it fear. Since we know that fear is the emotional response to threatened harm, and that it compels retreat, we are now in a position to deal with our fear from the position of a little more self-knowledge than we had before we learned its name.

Owning Feelings

Before we begin to shape a response to our fear, another small but extremely important intermediary step is needed. Owning it. Saying aloud that it is ours. No one else drove us to it, made us feel it, or forced us to have it. It is a response that we cannot blame on our background or attribute to someone else's treatment of us. Even if our fear response is *in relationship* to our background or to someone else, it is still our response and not theirs. It has occurred in the context of our personality and our body, a personality and a body unique enough to produce a variety of responses that someone else's personality and body might not produce under the same circumstances.

Owning a particular feeling can seem more real if we actually do say it aloud, particularly to ourselves, and possibly to another. "I am afraid." "I am feeling very frightened." Many people are surprised to realize how much that simple verbalization forces them to deal with their feelings. It is harder to repress or ignore something that has been spoken aloud.

65

Responding to Feelings

Sometimes, emotional reactions occur so fast that we can only act in a programmed fashion. This is particularly true when the issue is physical survival. If I am on the railroad tracks and suddenly I hear a train coming, the healthiest thing to do is react instantly to the threat and retreat. Reflecting on the situation first to clarify my feelings would indeed be absurd.

At other times the instantaneous expression of emotion is equally healthy, particularly when the situation seems to elicit a particular emotional response. If I am nonchalantly led into a darkened room, and suddenly the lights go on, and all my friends are there waving balloons and yelling "happy birthday," it is entirely appropriate to give full and immediate expression to my surprise.

Taking the time to reflect on our feelings before responding is obviously for those situations which offer a variety of possible responses, some of them healthy and some of them unhealthy, and which allow at least some time for thinking.

Thinking is key to responding, once the earlier processes of noticing, naming, and owning have been attended to adequately. Responding to our emotional experience requires thinking about the options. What choices do I have in response to my feelings? What can I do that would be most conducive to growth? Least conducive to growth? Is my instinctive response (running if I am afraid, attacking if I am angry) the most appropriate one for me under the circumstances? How will various possible responses affect the people in my life?

Sometimes the best response is easy to see. Other times it is not. Sometimes we can take as much time as we want to in order to discern. Other times we may have only enough time for a momentary reflection. However easy or difficult, and however much or little time there is, choosing our responses to emotional states is an effort to choose life.

Being attentive to our inner experience resembles biblical hovering. It is like hanging in the air, circling over our life, noticing, watching, attending. It involves entering into the rhythm of creation.

As people who remember a hovering God and tread the path of a passionate preacher from Nazareth, emotional awareness means more than survival. It means faithfulness—faithfulness to a potter.

4

NEVER LET THE SUN SET ON YOUR ANGER

Anger and Its Expression

Your mind must be renewed by a spiritual revolution so that you can put on the new self that has been created in God's way, in the goodness and holiness of the truth.
So from now on, there must be no more lies: *You must speak the truth to one another*, since we are all parts of one another. *Even if you are angry, you must not sin:* never let the sun set on your anger (Eph 4:23-26).

Immediately after the experience of Pentecost, the earliest followers of Jesus experienced overwhelming zeal and enthusiasm. Their energies were focused on preaching the reign of God and converting people to Jesus. Unbelievers were told about Jesus: how he lived, why he died, that he lived still and would come very soon in glory.

Even though the emphasis was on the missionary movement—getting out the word about Jesus—the earliest disciples and apostles never forgot that there was more to following than preaching. There was also living. There were relationships to be formed and communities to be built. From the beginning it was clear that those who were baptized considered themselves bound by profound responsibilities to one another. They were obligated to love one another, to treat one another as brothers and sisters.

It was never easy. As time went on communities grew both in size and number. Personal differences increased. Persecutions intensified. It became even harder to remember that being Christian made tough demands on a person's behavior in relationships. It was not enough to hear about Jesus. It was not enough to be plunged into the waters of baptism. It was not enough to pray and break bread in his name. Christians had to *live* their faith in the everyday give-and-take of relationships, relationships fraught with all of the emotional upheaval that you and I know.

By the time the letter to the Ephesians was written, Christian communities had settled in for the long haul. Years had come and gone without the advent of the parousia. The original apostles were dead. The excitement of the initial missionary movement had faded. The Christians at Ephesus were learning to live with routine. They had their jobs and their families. They had mediocrity. They had differences. And they had anger.

The author of Ephesians must have been familiar with situations among the Christians at Ephesus where anger had been expressed in sinful ways, ways that were not compatible with the "new self" that Christians are called to put on. The letter contains an invitation to renewal. It urges the Ephesians to shake themselves up, to get out of the rut of business-as-usual and take more seriously the gospel message of conversion. It calls them to enter into a serious process of personal growth. That "spiritual revolution," as the author of Ephesians calls it, is not more frequent prayer or more ardent meditation. It is a behavior change, a change in the words and actions of those who were "parts of one another." The Ephesians are called to a spirituality of interaction—of flesh and blood, face-to-face talking and acting.

The writer of the letter recognizes that the way individuals behave toward one another is intimately connected to spirituality. The way Christians interact reflects the level of conversion they have experienced. What they do when they become angry says something about the degree of holiness that lives in their hearts.

Spiritual renewal includes finding a way of expressing anger that is congruent with the holiness and truth to which all Christians are called. Genuine conversion, real spirituality, is not something we keep in the privacy of our hearts. It is not something that occurs in our souls. It is not confined to prayer. Authentic spirituality touches all of life. It gets into the nitty-gritty of relationships. It spills over into the words we speak and into the ways we interact with those around us. It influences what we do when we are happy, how we respond when we are jealous, where we go when we are restless. It mirrors itself in the ways we express anger.

The Search to Understand Anger

People have had troublesome experiences with anger since time began. It is an emotion that is uncomfortable and often painful. Sometimes it is confusing. The fact that it has such power is awesome both to those who feel it within themselves and to those who feel it from others. Because anger has the potential to affect human relationships so strongly, more discussion has centered around it than perhaps any other emotion.

Anger has been the subject of art, literature, philosophy, psychology and theology. It has been sculpted, painted, dramatized, defined and evaluated. Some have exulted it. Some have feared it. Some have denied it. Some have condemned it.

The Christian church has been at the center of history in the discussions surrounding anger. The church writings have never isolated the *feeling* of anger and condemned it; the operative definition used by those who included it in the list of capital sins included expression, presumably hurtful expression, of the feeling. Yet today it is recognized that the church leaders who defined anger as sinful did not have the benefit of contemporary understandings regarding the normalcy and importance of all human emotions. It is not surprising that there was never a distinction made between anger as a feeling (or emotion) and anger in relationship to its expression. This modern distinction, however, does not automatically enable people to feel suddenly comfortable with their anger. For the many Catholic Christians who have sincerely believed that the *feeling* of anger in itself constitutes sinfulness, it will take some time to develop an equally sincere belief that the feeling of anger is a normal human emotion, created by God, and given to us as a gift —a resource for physical and psychological survival. For the many who have learned to deny their anger for religious reasons, learning to express it in healthier ways will require concentrated effort. And for those who have spent years confessing their angry feelings with anonymous voices in little dark rooms, it will feel awkward to stand face to face in daylight relationships and speak words of anger aloud.

It Sounds As Though We Shouldn't Get Angry

Recently a Catholic priest who had experienced past difficulties with anger confided that the two previous years he had spent in a weekly therapy group had helped him overcome the powerful guilt he experienced whenever he felt angry—until he was praying the scriptures and read these words of Matthew:

> But I say this to you: anyone who is angry with his brother will answer for it before the court (Mt 5:22).

"I felt all of that old guilt start to stir and churn," he said. "Of course, I have had enough new learning experiences now so the guilt doesn't have the same hold over me, but I still get automatic twinges of uneasiness whenever I read anything in scripture that makes it sound as though we shouldn't get angry."

Like many who have difficulty with uncomfortable emotions, this priest had grown up in a home where he was not allowed to show any outward expression of anger. On more than a few occasions he had been severely punished for "getting mad." A religion teacher who frequently emphasized the relationship between getting angry and going to hell further solidified his childhood tendency to fear and repress anger. Years later, as a 35-year-old adult with a bleeding ulcer, he was forced to re-examine his beliefs about anger and to learn new ways of managing it in his life. It has not been easy for him, but very gradually he has come to know that his anger can be a friend, a helpful resource enabling him to clarify his life and relationships, rather than an enemy, eroding away at his stomach. He has learned to admit, to himself and to others, that he does in fact get angry.

Coming to grips with his own anger has made this man a much more effective minister. Before, he was not able to be helpful to people who had problems with anger. Now he is.

Anyone Who Gets Angry Will Answer for It

Scripture is, for many, equated with the literal voice of God. It is not uncommon to isolate one phrase and hear it out of context, often a phrase that taps a particularly sensitive area of a person's life. If Matthew says, "Anyone who is angry will answer for it" (Mt 5:22), then the person thinks God is saying: "Don't ever *get* angry. Anger is bad. You'll get punished if you get angry." Thus the guilt cycle is fueled for another round in the sensitive religious conscience.

It is important to remember that each of the evangelists had a particular theological purpose for saying what he said. To isolate one part of the message is to distort it. The topic of anger is mentioned several times in the Christian scriptures—always in a particular context by a writer with a particular purpose in mind. Nowhere do the Christian scriptures condemn the simple feeling of anger.

When Matthew suggests that anyone who gets angry with a brother or a sister will answer for it, his admonition must be taken in context. The context is the Sermon on the Mount. Matthew is anxious to convince his Jewish hearers that Jesus and his message are connected to the Jewish tradition, that Jesus has not come to abolish the Old Law. Jesus asks more of his followers than was asked of them in the Old Law without negating that Old Law. Matthew lists an elaborate series of things that were asked of the people in the Old Law and shows how Jesus asks this and more:

> "You have learnt how it was said to our ancestors: *You must not kill;* and if anyone does kill he must answer for it before the court. **But I say this to you: Anyone who is angry with his brother will answer for it before the court**" (Mt 5:21-22, emphasis added).

> "You have learnt how it was said: *Eye for eye and tooth for tooth.* **But I say this to you: Offer the wicked no resistance**" (Mt 5: 38-39, emphasis added).

> "You have learnt how it was said: *You must love your neighbor and hate your enemy.* **But I say this to you: Love your enemies and pray for those who persecute you**" (Mt 5: 43-44, emphasis added).

The Old Law asked a degree of love that was limited. The Israelites had to curtail their retaliatory responses. They couldn't kill, seek excessive revenge, or hate their neighbors. Jesus doesn't eliminate this, he adds to it. He takes the Old Law from limited love to expansive love. Matthew is dealing with human relationships and makes it clear that "being a follower of Jesus calls for a radically profound understanding of one's relationship to other people." Jesus' followers are not to seek revenge in any form, not even against their enemies and not even when they are angry.[13]

The word used for "angry" in this instance is the Greek *orgizō.* It can also be translated "wrath" or "rage." It suggests a degree of anger so strong that it could lead to violent expression. Matthew's Jesus is not say-ing don't ever *feel* any anger toward your brothers or sisters. He is saying don't let your anger get out of hand. Don't let it turn into the kind of rage that boils in your heart and leads you to retaliate. Avoiding exter-nal, overt violence, such as killing, is not enough. Christians must not *harbor* anger toward one another or let it drive them to any kind of hurtful expression.

A closer look at Matthew's reference to anger further clarifies that he is condemning the kind of anger or rage that compels a person to in-flict pain on another.

> "But I say this to you: anyone who is angry [filled with rage or wrath] with his brother will answer for it before the court; if a man calls his brother 'Fool' he will answer for it before the Sanhedrin; and if a man calls him 'Rene-gade' he will answer for it in hell fire" (Mt 5:22).

Matthew is clearly dealing with the kind of anger that seeks re-venge. To the Hebrew mentality calling another "fool" was particularly insulting. "Renegade" was a similar expression of abuse. The followers of Jesus must not only avoid killing each other physically, they must also avoid killing each other psychologically with verbal weapons. The Old Law condemned anger that led to murder. The New Law condemns an-ger that leads to psychological slaughter. It demands that Christians rid themselves of all those expressions of nursed anger that are geared to wound others: sarcastic statements, hostile silence, sharp remarks, put-downs, insults, temper outbursts, cold gestures. They must not harbor any form of anger that could lead them to negate the worth or diminish the value of any of their brothers and sisters.

Even If You Are Angry

The author of Ephesians understands anger in much the same way. It is not the *feeling* of anger that is wrong, but the hurtful or sinful be-havior that might come from it.

> *Even if you are angry [orgizō] you must not sin:* never let the sun set on your anger. . . . Never have grudges against others, or lose your temper, or raise your voice to anybody, or call each other names, or allow any sort of spitefulness (Eph 4:26, 31).

It is understood that people will experience feelings of anger toward one another. They will become provoked, irritated, and even filled with rage in some instances. But these feelings cannot lead to abusive behavior, to bearing grudges, or to any actions that shut others out with an unforgiving attitude.

There are several other places in the writings of the Christians where anger is specifically mentioned. In Colossians and James, its usage is similar to that of Ephesians.

> But now you, of all people, must give all these things up: getting angry, being bad-tempered, spitefulness, abusive language . . . (Col 3:8).

> Be *quick to listen* but *slow* to speak and slow to rouse your temper; God's righteousness is never served by man's anger (Jas 1:19-20).

Christians are bound by a New Law, a new way of *responding* to their anger. They, above all, should be examples of that new way in all dimensions of their lives. No longer are they to be people given to displays of anger that destroy the community and generate ongoing divisions.

Paul gives a similar caution to the Corinthians and Galatians. He uses a different Greek expression for anger, *thymos*, to make his point. It is a word that refers to a particularly strong, wrathful feeling toward someone. Some translations render *thymos* as "anger." The Jerusalem Bible translates it "roused tempers."

> What I am afraid of is that when I come . . . there will be wrangling, jealousy, and tempers roused [*thymos*], . . . backbiting and gossip . . . (2 Cor 12:20).

> When self-indulgence is at work the results are . . . feuds and wrangling, jealousy, bad temper [*thymos*] and quarrels; disagreements, factions . . . (Gal 5:19-20).

Here, as elsewhere in scripture where anger is mentioned along with other destructive behaviors, Paul is borrowing from an established list of Hellenistic vices. In the Greco-Roman world it was a common practice to compile lists to govern the behavior of people. The Hellenists had lists of virtues, lists of vices, lists of household rules. These were developed by Stoic philosophers quite apart from any kind of Christian influence. Because the lists were accessible and familiar to all, Christian writers often used them when they were advising Christians about how they should treat one another. They cautioned them to avoid the commonly held vices (wrangling, jealousy, bad tempers, quarrels, disagreements, factions) and to practice the commonly held virtues.

Paul, then, is not addressing anger as an emotion in isolation, nor is he suggesting that feeling angry is sinful. He is repeating the well-known list of Hellenistic vices to remind Christians to avoid those behaviors which even the pagans knew would be harmful to the household.

Biblical Anger in Perspective

In any of the Christian writings where reference is made to anger, the author is not dealing with it from a twentieth-century psychological perspective. As noted earlier, Paul and his contemporaries did not distinguish between the *experience* of anger as an emotion, and the *expression* of that anger in behavior. They probably did not know that repressed anger could be just as destructive to the individual as explosive anger was to the community. They did not understand the dynamics of repression at all since awareness of that concept had not yet occurred in history.

This does not mean that we cannot use psychological insights today in relating the scriptural message to our lives. It does mean, however, that we cannot read our contemporary psychological understandings back into scripture and assume that the sacred writers understood anger, and all the other emotions, in the same light that we do. What these writers did seem to know was that people had a tendency to vent anger in ways that were destructive. So they condemned anger without ever distinguishing between the inner feeling and its outward destructive expression.

Venting a Roused Spirit

What is the effect of unregulated rage? What can anger do to a community when it is unleashed without restraint? In its most violent form, uncontrolled anger can motivate wars, murder, assault, rape, and all forms of abuse that violate and destroy people. Many of the people who commit violent crimes against others are individuals who have a warehouse of stored anger, with a poor ability to regulate its expression or understand its force.

At other times, unregulated anger and rage stop short of inflicting physical damage. The violence is more emotional: refusing to talk to an other, sometimes for long periods; ignoring another deliberately; being verbally abusive; having temper outbursts; engaging in angry tirades; throwing things; slamming doors; holding grudges; pouting; engaging in martyr behavior; attempting to "get back" or "get even." All of these behaviors destroy relationships over time.

As long as these kinds of behaviors are used to deal with anger, interpersonal distance increases and relationships gradually break down and are sometimes severed altogether. Communities and families that live in an atmosphere where anger is dealt with in emotionally destructive ways are drained of energy and experience minimal closeness.

Contemporary Wrangling

If we look at our own families and communities, we see that the age-old tendency to express anger poorly is still with us. In too many homes anger speaks louder than love: Doors are slammed and fists are waved. Meals are eaten in tension. Television is watched in numb silence. Conversations end in shouting matches.

Too many lonely tears are sobbed into pillows at night. Too many houses are cleaned, too many reports are written, and too many ministries are served on unresolved anger energy. Too much food is eaten, too much alcohol is drunk, and too many pills are taken to keep the angers of our lives buried, yet nourished.

Do the ancient biblical words have anything significant to say to our contemporary wrangling?

Today, as nearly two thousand years ago, our families and our communities are divided by the effects of poorly expressed anger. There is behavior that sabotages the gospel and saps communities of the energy they need to witness to it.

To take seriously the words of Jesus, we may not be content to live passively in situations where anger is destroying relationships. We may not flip on the television set to ignore it, go to a meeting to escape it, or gossip to cope with it as the months and years go by.

What can we do? First, we can do more to understand the emotion of anger and learn to recognize its many manifestations in ourselves and in our environments. Second, we can identify our own patterns of dealing with anger. We can determine whether the way we deal with it is constructive or destructive. Finally, we can identify our options and choices in response to anger when it occurs in our lives. Throughout this entire process, it is important to keep in mind that anger is every bit as much a dynamic spiritual reality as it is a psychological one. To refuse to look at it is to refuse God's gift.

Looking At Anger Scientifically

How can we allow psychology to assist us as we attempt to look at anger in its full creational goodness and rich spiritual potential? Behavioral scientists have been studying anger, as well as the other emotions, for a long time. As early as 1872, Charles Darwin published his classic book, *The Expression of the Emotions in Man and Animals.* Studying anger responses in both humans and animals, Darwin observed some strong relationships. He suggested that baring fangs, snarling, and uttering savage sounds in dogs and cats was related to sneering and saying verbally abusive things in human adults.[14] In 1890 the American psychologist William James noticed that all emotions had physiological correlates. For example, when an individual experienced the emotion of anger, the body reacted automatically by increasing the pulse, elevating the blood pressure, quickening respirations, and secreting specific chemicals that produced other changes from head to toe.[15]

Research into human emotion has intensified in recent years. With regard to anger, we now know a number of things that can make it easier to understand and deal with in our lives.

The Anger Cycle

As mentioned in the previous chapter, anger in its most rudimentary form serves a survival function, as do all of the other emotions. *Anger, specifically, leads a person to destroy barriers to the satisfaction of some important need.* If, for example, I am on the brink of starvation, and someone else attempts to take away the only food I have left, I will become angry because something I need for survival is threatened. My anger will generate energy that mobilizes my whole body for attack: my muscles will tighten; my pulse will increase bringing extra blood to my muscles, joints and bones; my blood pressure will rise; my respiratory rate will speed up. All of my attention will be focused on removing the barrier. I will lunge forward toward the person, knock him or her down, retrieve my food. My basic need for food has now been satisfied. My muscles will relax. My pulse and respirations will slow down. My blood pressure will return to normal. My attention will be directed elsewhere. My anger has helped me to survive physically. It can leave.

Anger, then, has played an important role in the evolution and physical survival of the human species. When barriers to food, water, shelter, mating and safety presented themselves, anger gave human beings energy to attack the barrier, destroy or remove it, and survive. The cycle of anger looks like this:

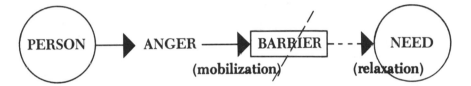

This same primitive anger cycle operates today in poverty situations, war zones and Third World countries. When dictators, governments and the powerful rich interfere with the satisfaction of basic needs for large populations of people, they constitute barriers—barriers which automatically generate a great deal of anger energy on the part of those who are deprived of their basic needs.

Why are there revolutions in Latin America? strikes in Poland? revolts in the Middle East? Because the satisfaction of basic needs is being denied to large populations of people. They are hungry. They have no land and no power. They live in squalor without minimally adequate shelter. They have diseases and no medicine. They live in constant fear of abduction and torture. They sleep with the sound of gunfire in the distance. Their basic survival is threatened. They are angry. They have to be angry. That is how God's gift functions. It is a fairly basic psychological equation, but one which seems to have passed by the understanding of many heads of governments.

When we know that most crimes of violence are committed by very angry people, it is not surprising that the crime rate is the highest in locations where poverty is greatest. The best way to reduce crime is not to punish the criminals, but to get at the source of their anger, that is, reduce the poverty that denies the satisfaction of basic needs and increase the therapeutic programs that help people learn more effective ways to express their anger and meet their needs. In most recent instances in this

77

country we have done just the opposite: increased the poverty level and reduced the therapeutic resources.

The anger response of those people who live without adequate food and housing, who dwell in conditions that spawn violence, and who reside in neighborhoods where they fear for their basic safety, is always being aroused. It creates a volatile energy source. When a person's body is constantly ready to attack and attacking fails to remove the barriers to his or her basic needs, anger only increases—until finally the individual is worn out and apathy sets in.

The Physiology of the Anger Response

If the emotion of anger did not trigger major physiological reactions, the human body would not have the strength or power it needs to remove barriers. This is particularly true when those barriers require physical destruction or removal. However, even when there are no physical barriers, the physiology of the anger response is still the same:

Physiology of the Anger Response

1. A *stimulus* occurs in the environment or in the individual.

— someone says an angry word
— someone gets a job I wanted
— I am ignored by another
— my food is taken away

2. The stimulus enters the cerebral cortex through the senses and is *perceived* and *interpreted*. Each person interprets (and therefore reacts) differently to a stimulus. Interpretation is influenced by:

— personality traits and genetic characteristics
— pattern of dealing with anger learned in childhood
— current level of need satisfaction
— physical condition
— degree of stored anger from the past
— personal beliefs, values and choices

3. Neurosecretory substances *activate the hypothalamus* in the base of the brain (the hypothalamus influences the physiological responses of the body).

4. The hypothalamus secretes a chemical which *activates the pituitary gland* in the brain.

5. The pituitary gland secretes the hormone *ACTH* into the bloodstream.

6. ACTH travels through the bloodstream and stimulates the *adrenal glands* (situated above the kidneys) to *secrete adrenaline and cortisone* into the blood. These hormones then stimulate the various changes that prepare the body to fight.

> — pupils dilate, making them more sensitive to light (this response is visible to the sensitive observer)
>
> — respiratory rate increases and breathing becomes shallow
>
> — heart pumps faster, increasing the pulse
>
> — blood vessels constrict, elevating the blood pressure
>
> — blood is diverted away from the digestive system and sent to the muscles (many people who have prolonged anger also have chronic constipation for this reason)
>
> — muscles tighten throughout the body (results in neck and shoulder soreness and low back pain if prolonged)

Whether we get angry because someone has placed a barrier between us and our food, or because we need recognition and someone else (barrier) gets it, makes no difference. The physiological reaction in the body is still the same. Emotions, then, touch off specific physiological chain reactions in the body that are automatic. We have looked at those reactions with reference to the emotion of anger. However, while the experience of different emotions leads to different external responses (exploration for anticipation, running for fear, attack for anger, cooperating for joy, crying for sadness, affiliating and self-assertion for acceptance, rejecting for disgust and stopping and reorienting for surprise), the general physiology is the same for all emotional reactions. All involve perception of a stimulus followed by readying of the body to do something. We can deny a feeling, such as anger, or we can even be unaware of being angry, but our body knows—and doesn't forget.

Diagram of the Anger Response

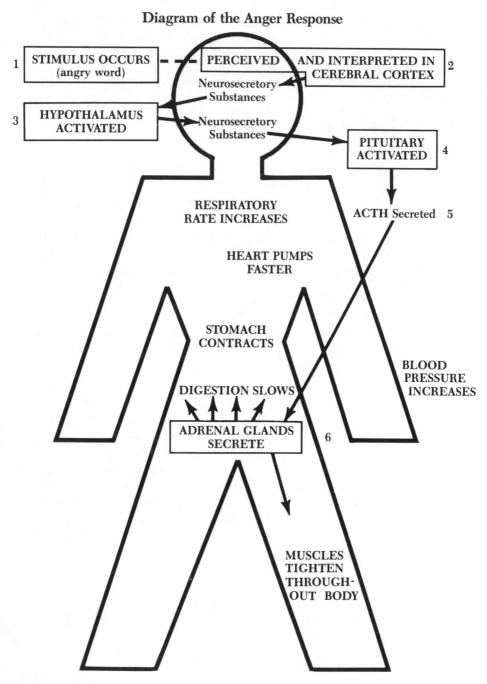

1 STIMULUS OCCURS (angry word)

PERCEIVED AND INTERPRETED IN CEREBRAL CORTEX 2

Neurosecretory Substances

3 HYPOTHALAMUS ACTIVATED

Neurosecretory Substances

PITUITARY ACTIVATED 4

RESPIRATORY RATE INCREASES

ACTH Secreted 5

HEART PUMPS FASTER

STOMACH CONTRACTS

BLOOD PRESSURE INCREASES

DIGESTION SLOWS

ADRENAL GLANDS SECRETE 6

MUSCLES TIGHTEN THROUGH-OUT BODY

When Being Angry Doesn't Work

In an earlier example, the person used anger energy to remove a barrier to food and that person's body then returned to its normal relaxed state. But using anger energy is not always that simple, particularly under some of the following circumstances:

— I know I am angry but I don't know why. I don't know the name of the need that is being blocked.

— My needs are self-indulgent or out of proportion so my anger is aroused easily and often.

— I have unmet needs from my childhood of which I am unaware.

— The barrier to my need is someone or something that I cannot eliminate or diminish from my life.

— I don't have access to the barrier (person) who is blocking my need.

— I am afraid to confront the barrier (person) who is blocking my need.

— I have erected unnecessary barriers, or I have perceived barriers that do not exist.

— I have stored anger in my body from the past.

— I have learned unhealthy ways to deal with my anger.

In all of these situations the physiological response to anger can be prolonged either because we have not given adequate expression to our anger, or because we have evoked the anger response when we do not really need it. When anger does not lead to some kind of health-promoting action, it serves no purpose and may be harmful. When we become angry and do not act in some constructive way in response to it, our bodies stay mobilized to fight, even without our conscious awareness. If it is not directed toward a real barrier, it will be directed toward something—or someone—else. It will fight.

Some of the physical signs of prolonged anger mobilization include restlessness and insomnia, physical illness, sexual dysfunction, appetite gain or loss, depression, tearfulness, irritability, problems concentrating and fatigue.

Many studies have shown, and continue to show, that poorly handled anger can lead to a variety of debilitating physical symptoms and diseases. Ulcers, migraines, tension headaches, some forms of arthritis, skin disorders (eczema, hives, rashes), tics, asthma, low back pain, neck and shoulder pain, colitis, spastic colon, chronic constipation or diarrhea, and vascular disease all have strong links to prolonged anger mobilization. The problem is that the body systems were not meant to store anger. The stomach, for example, was created to hold food, not anger. When we use it as a storehouse for anger energy, it will eventually rebel. For the individual who has any of these conditions, particularly more than one of them, it might be helpful to look for hidden anger.

The physical signs and symptoms that occur under states of prolonged emotional mobilization have their basis in the chemical reactions of the body. For example, the individual who is chronically fearful or angry often has symptoms of weakness, fatigue and lethargy. Some researchers have demonstrated that adrenaline, which is released into the bloodstream during emotional arousal and usually effects an increase in energy, actually has the opposite effect when the mobilization is prolonged. Eventually, adrenaline interferes with glucose and oxygen utilization by the muscles, producing a sensation of tiredness.[16]

Taking medicine to relieve uncomfortable symptoms, particularly if a physical examination has revealed no organic cause for the disorder, may do more than distract us from anger. It may blunt revelation.

Some people deal with pent-up anger not physically, but psychologically. They manage to avoid serious physical symptoms by releasing their anger energy in spurts or in subtle, camouflaged ways. Dorothy Heiderscheit, OSF, says that this is characteristic of people who have a lot of anger energy that is never fully acknowledged. It is turned into what she terms "free floating hostility," a constant undercurrent of anger that reveals itself in tone of voice, facial expressions, body movements and behavior. A person experiencing free floating hostility is:

— quick to notice the faults of others

— negative and critical

— extremely demanding of self and others

— excessively competitive at sports, volatile and visibly angry at losing

— argumentative, unwilling to give in, determined to be right

— hypersensitive to criticism and others' remarks

— rounded through the shoulders with an elevation in the center of the shoulders below the neck (anger hump)

— quick to verbally lash out at others, accusing them, correcting them, interrupting their attempts to talk

— tearful, cries easily when talking

— likely to tell the same stories of past hurts and disappointments over and over; telling them doesn't seem to be productive

— saccharine, overly sweet, overly complimentary

— a nervous talker, carries on constant commentary

— quick to lose his or her temper over small things

— sarcastic in tone of voice

— a holder of grudges, can forgive but not forget

— likely to speak of his or her anger while smiling or laughing

— jerky, particularly in movements of the head and hands

Individuals who show these behaviors are often unaware of them. The behaviors are much more apt to be apparent to others. They are clues that the individual is holding a slow-burning, constant fire within that is keeping the fight response mobilized. The fight is carried on with words and gestures, and the person never confronts the underlying cause of the anger and may not even know it is there. Usually such individuals have difficulties in relationships. They are either in fairly constant conflict with others, or else others tend not to want to be around them leaving them feeling hurt, lonely and growing angrier.

Anger Will Have Its Say

Both anger-related physical illness and anger-induced behavioral tendencies tell us an important fact about anger: When anger is present, particularly if it is intense or of long-standing duration, it will automatically be expressed. Sooner or later it will show itself in our bodies, in our facial expressions, in our tone of voice, in our mannerisms, and in our way of treating others. We cannot be angry and assume that no one will know, or that it won't show. Consequently we do not have a choice between expressing our anger and not expressing it. It will be expressed. What we do have a choice about, however, is *how* it will be expressed.

5

ZEAL FOR YOUR HOUSE WILL DEVOUR ME

Anger and the Quest For Transcendence

If anger, in its most elemental sense, is an emotion necessary for survival, how and why is it operative in those instances where basic survival is not threatened? Why do people get angry—sometimes angry enough to kill—when they are safe, fed and warm? Why are they sometimes stirred to attack when they are experiencing no threat to their survival?

Jesus was a person, John the evangelist tells us, who was moved to such an anger:

> And in the Temple he found people selling cattle . . . , and the money changers sitting at their counters there. Making a whip out of some cord, he drove them all out of the Temple, . . . scattered the money changers' coins, knocked their tables over and said. . . , "Take all this out of here and stop turning my Father's house into a market." Then his disciples remembered the words of scripture: *Zeal for your house will devour me* (Jn 2:14-17).

Jesus was not in any personal danger when he entered the Temple court in the story. He had no immediate needs that were being deprived. Or did he? Was there a need beyond the basic ones that roused his anger and fired him to attack? These questions move us to look at anger in a broader sense.

The Human Needs That Anger Serves

We know that we have psychological and spiritual needs as well as physical ones. We also know that the psychological needs become more important as physiological needs are satisfied. A person who is lost in the desert without water will be motivated by physiological needs—satisfying thirst and finding safety. Such a person will not be concerned about feeling accepted or achieving status. Once out of the desert, however, acceptance and achievement needs will become more important.

Abraham Maslow has provided a schema for understanding the motivational force of all of our needs that is still widely accepted by behavioral scientists. Most people today are familiar with Maslow's hierarchy of needs as they relate to the quest for self-actualization. What they are perhaps less familiar with is the important relationship between anger and the quest for self-transcendence.

Anger can be a powerful source of energy, enabling us to confront anything which destroys the Temple of God's people, if we have properly claimed it and directed it. On the other hand, it can be just as powerful as a stumbling block, keeping us tightly focused on ourselves, if we have held on to it. Let us see how.

While not everyone agrees that satisfying needs is the only source of motivation in people, most agree that it is a powerful one, and plays a greater role in the behavioral motivation of those whose past needs have not been adequately met. Psychologists know well that people who have not had their basic needs for love met as children will continue to seek love, sometimes in unhealthy ways, as adults. Satisfying that essential need for love and acceptance will play an important role in motivating much of their adult behavior.

Because anger is the specific emotion linked to the deprivation of need satisfaction, familiarity with Maslow's schema is important:[17]

According to Maslow's research with healthy adults, all people have essentially the same basic needs which tend to be met in a hierarchical fashion. Physiological needs must be met in order for the individual to move on to meeting safety needs. When both physiological and safety needs are satisfied, needs for acceptance arise and occupy the person's attention. Once these are reasonably met, the person seeks to meet growing esteem needs. Originally Maslow believed that self-actualization, or reaching one's full potential, was at the top of the scale and

SELF-TRANSCENDENCE (Genuine Holiness)
/\

The ability to move beyond one's own needs, often in dramatic ways, to serve needs of others. It is difficult to reach this stage in a genuine way unless other needs have been reasonably met. The concept of self-transcendence is more recent.

SELF-ACTUALIZING NEEDS: Being able to reach one's potential, developing one's gifts, integration.

ESTEEM NEEDS: Feeling important, useful, competent, needed.

ACCEPTANCE NEEDS: Having love, friends, intimacy, feeling a part of other people's lives.

SAFETY NEEDS: Security, stability, freedom from fear.

PHYSIOLOGICAL NEEDS: Food, water, shelter, sex, whatever is needed for survival. If a person does not meet these needs, he or she will not be able to move on to the next level of need.

the final need group to be met. However, Maslow and several researchers since him recognized that the original hierarchy of needs didn't explain all human behavior.

Beyond Self-Actualization

What motivates the firefighter who runs into a burning building, neglecting her own safety needs, to save another person? What motivates a starving father to give his only cup of rice to his child? What motivated Oscar Romero or Jean Donovan and her friends to stay in a life-threatening situation in El Salvador and continue to speak out when they knew it could cost them their lives? What motivated Jesus? Why did he lash out at the Temple sellers when their actions were not personally threatening to him?

If Jesus was a human being with the same safety, acceptance, esteem and self-actualizing needs that we have, why did he continue to say the things that he knew would increasingly alienate him from the religious establishment? Why did he continue to talk about a kingdom of equality when it cost him the acceptance of the crowds? Where was his need for esteem, his normal desire to feel competent in his ministry and important to people, as he hung blood-stained and publicly humiliated on the cross?

His story and the stories of other heroic sons and daughters of God have told us that there is something more than need satisfaction that motivates human beings. Maslow himself recognized a motivational force higher than self-actualization, an inner drive to place the needs of others above a person's own needs. Some have called it self-transcendence. Others have called it personal integration. Still others have called it holiness. Jesus called it love.

Self-Transcendence in Action

Whatever name we give it, we know that when it is operative in even one human being, good news is proclaimed to the poor, liberty is brought to captives, the blind have new sight, the downtrodden are set free, and people feel favored by God.

The person capable of self-transcendence, the person who is able to create a life-giving, freeing environment for others, the person who is most ready to receive God's gift of holiness, is most frequently the person who has experienced adequate past satisfaction of basic needs so that those needs no longer have the motivational force that they once had. Such people usually have experienced themselves as good and worthwhile persons. They have been accepted by others, have developed close friendships, and have known intimacy. They have experienced some success, feel competent in some areas of their lives, and know their lives reflect growth. They have been able to accept pain as an inevitable part of that growth.

To what degree do needs have to be satisfied in order for an individual to experience increasing integration? That is a difficult question to answer because it is not possible to accurately measure needs or their level of satisfaction. Also, since people have infinite uniqueness and individuality, the degree of need satisfaction required for each person varies. It is easier to see the *effects* of both need satisfaction and need deprivation because both show themselves in behavior.

Need Deprivation in Action

We have looked at some of the characteristics of people whose needs have been adequately met in childhood and have identified such people as most capable of eventual self-transcendence. But what happens to those whose needs have not been adequately tended? Usually, unless there has been some form of therapeutic intervention, need-deprived people become stuck at a particular need level. The unmet needs from that level intensify and stimulate unconcious need-seeking adult behavior:

Unmet Need	Characteristic Adult Behavior
Physiological Needs	Hoarding, "pack-rat" behavior, frugal, chronic anxiety, easily frustrated, difficulty sharing, overly focused on some physiological need (food, environment)
Safety Needs	Fear of separation or physical harm, rigid, clings to what is familiar, fights change, finds moving very difficult and adjusts slowly to moves, feels rootless, helpless, fearful, can't take risks, can't tolerate ambiguity, dependent
Acceptance Needs	Chronic loneliness, feels alienated, strange, not really part of a group, clinging in friendship, may do things to get attention, frequent illnesses and hospitalizations, low self-esteem, sometimes

seems shallow or phoney to others, problems trusting people, preoccupied with
finding a friend, fitting in somewhere,
may try to use ministry or parenthood to
meet needs to be needed, doting

Esteem Needs_____Secretly compares self to others, competitive, feels inferior, often jealous, may be
controlling in relationships, daydreams
about great accomplishments, exagger-
ates accomplishments, seeks prestige,
power, recognition, often can't follow
through with responsibilities when power
is attained, may overachieve to prove self,
may attempt to do something he or she
lacks capacity for, likes to be in the limelight, may seem insensitive to others'
needs or very narcissistic

Self-Actualization_____Feels restless, unfulfilled, dissatisfied with
self, bored, has regrets about life, may
become bitter, negative, searching, aloof

Self-Transcendence_____Self-indulgent, overly focused on self,
brags about accomplishments in life,
never satisfied, selfish, careless, restless,
sense of emptiness, may always be "on
the go" to fill the void or may become a
loner

Physiological, safety and acceptance needs are critical to infancy
and early childhood development. If met, they fade in importance as
primary motivators of behavior. The child will still need to feel loved
but will not unconsciously act in ways designed to get love, since the
feeling and experience of love is there and can be counted upon. Esteem
needs grow in importance beginning in early childhood and continue
throughout adolescence. Self-actualization and self-transcendence needs
usually do not emerge until young adulthood and continue throughout
life.

Whenever an individual is trying to satisfy basic needs at any level,
and is blocked from doing so, the anger response will be evoked.

Forced Self-Transcendence

If we are adults, and self-transcendence reflects the level of adult integration that enables us to put the needs of others ahead of our own needs, then shouldn't we forget about our own needs, even if they haven't been met? Aren't lingering needs for acceptance, esteem and self-actualization merely manifestations of selfishness in an adult? Isn't attempting to meet them a form of self-centeredness? If we were truly holy, wouldn't we forget about meeting our own needs and concentrate on serving others?

In the past, popular spirituality would have answered yes to all of these questions. Focusing attention on ourself and our own personal growth was often viewed in direct opposition to genuine spirituality. Many sincere people have tried, and are still trying, to live in self-transcendence without ever getting to know the self they are transcending. That is something like starting a swimming career with backward flips off the high board—before learning to swim. It demands skill not yet acquired. It requires a degree of integration not yet attained.

When we consciously try to move to the level of self-transcendence by engaging in behaviors which are characteristic of that level—other centeredness, service, self-giving—before we have adequately moved through and come to know our needs at other levels, what kind of things happen?

— I go to Appalachia to serve the needs of the poor and my own unmet and unacknowledged need for security causes me to be rigid, fearful, dissatisfied—more of a burden than a help to those I am serving.

— I get married and my own unmet need for acceptance drives me to jealous outbursts and constant demands for attention from my husband.

— I become a priest and my own unmet need for stability compels me to cling to old traditions, to be controlling, to tenaciously fight renewal.

— I have children and my own unmet need to be needed leads me to be possessive and to keep them dependent on me. They grow up as broken as I am.

— I become a parish minister and my own unmet need for esteem pushes me to compete with others on the team, to resist their ideas and to be threatened by their successes.

91

— I accept a supervisory position and my own unmet need for prestige causes me to be critical, demanding and insensitive toward those with whom I work.

And then what happens? Instead of service, instead of genuine self-transcendence, there is anger. A great deal of anger. Anger in Appalachia. Anger in marriages. Anger in the church. Angry children. Angry parish teams. Angry organizations. And anger in us—anger and a whole host of other uncomfortable, confusing feelings because our leap to transcendence, our effort to be for others, hasn't worked. The very people we have attempted to serve and to love have in fact become *barriers* to the fulfillment of our own deeper needs. The poor only intensify my insecurity. I sense a power and a nobility in them that I cannot even name and it threatens me to the core. . . . My husband cannot begin to fill the huge void in my life by himself. . . . Church renewal is a threat to my personal stability and sense of control. . . . My children rebel and I feel even less needed and even more of a failure. . . . The parish team stands in the way of my recognition. . . . The organization will not let me use it so I can feel important.

These examples do not suggest that we put our lives on hold and eliminate all efforts to serve others until we have satisfied our own needs. But they do suggest that we should not attempt to get married, have children, enter ministry situations, live in community, become ordained, or accept any kind of service or leadership position without knowing ourselves, without first becoming aware of the need level at which we are functioning. Why? Because past unmet needs will continue to press to be met. If we do not know what they are, we will unconsciously attempt to meet our needs, sometimes in unhealthy ways and sometimes at the expense of others, no matter how good our intentions are.

Giving a Name to Our Needs

How can we know if our needs have been adequately satisfied? Adequately enough so that we will not hurt and use others in our veiled attempts to appease their pull?

We can listen—to our lives, to our behavior, to our bodies, to our feelings. We can begin to notice what is happening in our relationships. Persistent, chronic feelings of fear, anxiety, insecurity, inadequacy, dependency, passivity, jealousy, loneliness, and anger can all be signals that we are stuck at a particular need level.

This is one of the ways that feelings can be sources of divine revelation to us—they call our attention to our lives. They ask us to take a deeper look at what is happening and at what is missing. They give us clues to the areas of our lives that need further growth and integration. They invite us to let our hidden selves grow strong. They represent God's intervention. They are moments of grace.

If we learn to know what needs are apt to be motivating our behavior, then we can reflect on those needs and find appropriate ways to more adequately meet them rather than impose them haphazardly and unreflectively on others.

Human Needs: A Reflection of God's Image

We are children of a potter, a divine artisan who has fashioned us with hunger and thirst, a need to feel safe, a desire to be accepted, a yearning for intimacy. It is according to the wish of the potter that we feel good about ourselves, that we develop the gifts that lie within us, that we progress and grow and reach our greatest potential, and that we do it not in isolation but as brothers and sisters. That potter has given us powerful drives and deep longings and filled us with dreams. And called it good.

Our ordinary needs, then, are not selfish. They are in the image of God. They express the wild creativity of a potter. Fulfilling them can move us toward self-transcendence. Acknowledging them can lead us to holiness, a holiness that rests on a deep appreciation and knowledge of who we are. It is only when our basic needs are not met that they can grow to disproportionate size and assume greater importance than intended. It is only when they are not met that they eat away at us and drive us to engage in behavior that is disruptive to relationships. It is only when they are not met that we erect barriers where there needn't be any, barriers that evoke the anger response and send us into a whirlwind of fighting.

If early *need deprivation* can cause us to become over-focused on meeting our needs later in life, so can excessive *need satisfaction*. If we are over-fed, over-protected and over-indulged, our expectations for fulfillment and satisfaction as adults will be excessively high. We will be spoiled, hard to please, and certainly a good distance away from self-transcendence.

Both deprivation and indulgence, then, interfere with the normal role that needs play in motivating adult behavior. Both distort the vision of the potter. It is not the ordinary, reasonable satisfaction of needs that is selfish. To the contrary, it is precisely their adequate satisfaction that frees us from self-absorption and anxiety and enables us to let go of our own needs to serve those of others.

People who stand out in history as those who have given selflessly of themselves, who have sacrificed their lives, who have performed amazing deeds of heroism in behalf of others, are those who have been able to transcend themselves. *Ordinarily* they have been able to do this because their past lives and childhood relationships brought them the love, self-esteem and sense of competence that freed them from self-preoccupation and propelled them outward toward others.

Self-Transcendence and Jesus

The early Christians understood Jesus as one who grew in wisdom and grace. That is simply a biblical way of saying that he grew physically, psychologically and spiritually. He learned to feel loved, accepted and secure. He developed a good self-concept, had a sense of competence and an ability to take risks. He had goals and dreams, and a desire to accomplish them. As he grew older, he had an intensified sense of purpose and mission. His need to bring it to completion was strong:

> "I have come to bring fire to the earth, and how I wish it were blazing already! There is a baptism I must still receive, and how great is my distress till it is over [*teleō*]!" (Lk 12:49-50).

The Greek *teleō* is translated "over." It actually means "accomplish" or "finish." It tells us that there was something that Jesus had to do, *needed* to accomplish, before he would be satisfied.

Here in this story we get a glimpse of the raw humanness of Jesus of Nazareth. His sense of purpose pushed him on, even drove him. He could not turn back on what he had to do no matter how much distress it brought him. What he had to do was not act out a scene in the drama of salvation. What he had to do was follow his dream. His need to actualize his vision was more powerful than his need to be safe, or accepted, or esteemed.

Jesus dreamed of a kingdom of love and equality. He *needed* to share that dream. Proclaiming the kingdom was his pathway to self-actualization. Jesus reached his full potential as he preached, and healed, and loved. He even fulfilled something of his own dream as he wrestled with the tensions of the "already" and "not yet" of the kingdom. It is here that self-actualization and self-transcendence converge.

At some point in Jesus' life his own burning need to bring the kingdom into people's lives was no longer his own need. It was no longer the vision of the reign of God or his own driving sense of purpose that kept him going. It was not the convictions he arrived at in the wilderness, or the long nights in prayer, or even the knowledge that his word was the word of God that made his life make sense. It was the awareness that everything that he did was really "for them," for the brothers and the sisters, the sons and the daughters of the living God, that gave final articulation to the self-transcendence of Jesus' life.

> As you sent me into the world,
> I have sent them into the world,
> and for their sake I consecrate myself
> so that they too may be consecrated in truth (Jn 17:18-19).

Then he could totally let go. Let go of his zeal for the kingdom. Let go of his sense of mission. Even let go of those he so loved. He could stop slipping away from the authorities. He could stop hoping to convince them of the kingdom. He could suffer without bitterness. He could die without anger because no one had taken anything away from him that he needed.

Self-transcendence is characterized by maximum letting go. It is not other-centered service as much as it is the recognition that only God can heal the pain and meet the needs and fill the void in human lives.

Jesus transcended his own human needs by going through them, by meeting them. He did not begin his public life with a dramatic display of self-sacrifice. He began it feeling lonely in the desert. He began it needing friends and companions. He began it searching the Old Law for a clue to his own purpose in life.

Always, he had needs—needs for food, needs for friendship, needs for solitude, needs to accomplish his mission. His needs were never overbalanced or self-indulgent. Nor were they denied. He cared for others even as he cared for himself. His love for others seemed to flow out of his own abundant love and not out of his deprivation.

His were ordinary human needs. The quality of parenting he had, the kinds of choices he made, the clarity of his sense of purpose, his frequent reflection, the expansiveness of his dreams, his receptivity to God's action in his life—all of this carried him beyond himself to complete transcendence—to full and final identification with others "for their sake."

That is how one usually arrives at self-transcendent behavior. At least that seems to be the way God acted in Jesus and the way God acts in most human beings.

Sometimes God Gets Dramatic

There are exceptions, however. At some times, in some places, and in some people, God acts outside of the usual pattern. At some times, and in some places, people are able to behave in dramatically self-transcendent ways even when their past needs have been woefully deprived. In these instances people jump into self-transcendence without traveling through earlier levels of growth.

They have been starving all of their lives, but they give bread to their children. They have never known safety, but they run into enemy gunfire to save a friend. They have never felt accepted, but they take courageous public stands that are sincere and real. They have always felt inadequate, but they stand proud and unthreatened before a rival's accomplishment. They take risks. They deny their own basic needs. They let go of jealousy. They have unexplainable courage in adversity. Sometimes they die. Why do they do it? What motivates them? How can they be so self-transcendent when they have been so deprived?

To think that we can find a reasonable explanation for all human behavior is arrogant. Psychology can help us a great deal in understanding ourselves, but it cannot regulate God's surprises.

If it is presumptuous to try to force God to act within the categories that we can define and understand, it is equally presumptuous to assume that we can, by our own initiative and by our own design, jump out of our human skins and short-circuit our human needs in search of personal transcendence. We cannot explain unusual expressions of transcendence. Nor can we set out to acquire transcendence for ourselves. We can neither control nor pursue great holiness. We can only receive it as a gift.

We can, however, make ourselves receptive to that gift by entering fully into the task of personal growth. We can set out on the journey laid out for us by the potter—the ordinary journey that takes us deeply into the human, deeply into flesh. A journey that will fill us with ambition and give us dreams. A journey that will make us excited and lonely and joyful and zealous. A journey that will acquaint us with our limitations and show us the cross. A journey that will sometimes carry us beyond our biggest dreams and let us know the experience of self-transcendent love.

Anger: A Companion to Personal Growth

A companion along that journey will be anger. It was there for Jesus, and it will be there for us. It can be an enemy, damaging bodies, disrupting relationships, and destroying families and communities. Or it can be there as a friend.

If we learn to recognize the physiological and psychological signs that accompany anger, it will be less likely to slip unnoticed and unintended into our behavior. Rather, it will serve as a beacon of self-knowledge and an energy source for action. Examining the things that evoke anger in us can tell us something about the kinds of needs that we have. It can lead us to review our life. It can help us to name the barriers to our needs and to come to know whether those barriers are real or imagined, old or new, erected by circumstances beyond our control or erected unnecessarily by ourselves.

Clarifying our deepest needs and being able to know the barriers to them puts us in the position of taking charge of our anger instead of it taking charge of us. If we know that we are angry, if we have some of the signs and symptoms of stored anger, then we can choose appropriate responses to that anger. Some of these responses will be discussed in a following chapter on conflict in relationships.

Quest for the Kingdom

In one of the scenes in Mark's gospel Jesus becomes angry with his disciples for interfering with his ministry. He expresses his anger quite directly:

> People were bringing little children to him, for him to touch them. The disciples turned them away, but when Jesus saw this he was indignant and said to them, "Let the little children come to me; do not stop them; for it is to such as these that the kingdom of God belongs" (Mk 10:13-14).

Did Jesus get irritated? Did he experience annoyance at seemingly insignificant issues? It appears that he did. But this story is not told so that Mark's audience would know that Jesus got as vexed as the next person when something important to him met interference. Nor is the story told to prove how much Jesus loved children.

Mark's Jesus had been talking with the crowds about the kingdom. While he was talking, people began to bring children to him to be touched. The disciples apparently saw the children and their need to be touched as bothersome, and they attempted to turn them away. Their rejection of the children is symbolic; they are turning away helpless, powerless, needy people, those who have just begun their process of personal growth, those whose strongest needs at this time are for acceptance.

And Jesus became angry, angry because the disciples still didn't understand that the kingdom doesn't reject imperfect, unfinished, even bothersome people. It embraces them. And so he put his arms around the children. He affirmed their child level of growth. He hugged their needs. He held all the yearning of their hearts to his. And he said that it is precisely to them that the kingdom belongs.

And what of all of the rest of God's children—insecure adults trying to feel at home, aging women and men still searching for acceptance; people too old to bounce on your lap needing so badly to be held? What about all of the needy people, those with poor self-esteem and failed dreams? Those who limp through life doing their best to care for others when their own lives reflect such deprivation? What about those who try to slip into the crowd, claim a place of importance, and feel blessed, even for a moment?

It is to such as these that the kingdom belongs.

6

HAVE CARE FOR ONE ANOTHER

Caring As an Expression of Christian Communication

One of the earliest admonitions that Paul gave the Christians was that they have genuine reverence for one another. He used the analogy of the body to remind them that care for the members of the community was rooted in God's creational intention and expressed in the design of the human body:

> But God has so composed the body, . . . that the members
> may have the same care for one another (1 Cor 12:24-25,
> RSV).

It was Paul's conviction that Christians are members of the body of Christ in much the same way as physical parts are related to the entire body. Christians are to one another, and to the whole community, as arms and legs are to one another and to the whole physical body. They are to be as close, as needed, and as much a part of one another as the various body parts are to the individual. It is having care that bonds Christians and deepens their identity as members of Christ's body.

In 1 Corinthians 12:25 the word used to describe this reality is the Greek *merimnaō* meaning "to care for." The word also means "to be anxious for." It is an ambiguous Greek word used to express solicitude or disquiet. It is found frequently in the Christian scriptures, often to warn against having the kind of preoccupying anxiety that prevents freedom in Christ:

"Martha, Martha," he said "you worry and fret [*merimnaō*] about so many things" (Lk 10:41).

While Jesus condemns cares that cause unnecessary anxiety, Paul's use of *merimnaō* suggests that the intense care Christians should have toward one another ought to be a source of legitimate anxiety. "If one part is hurt," Paul argues, "all parts are hurt with it" (1 Cor 12:26). By analogy, if someone within the Christian community is hurting, then that pain should affect other members of the community. While Christians should not be anxious about (*merimnaō*) superficial or insignificant things that distract them from the kingdom, they should be anxious about (*merimnaō*) their hurting and oppressed brothers and sisters.

Caring for others in this manner is not simply a polite gesture or a dispassionate offer of assistance. Nor is it seasonal. Preparing an annual Thanksgiving basket for the needy is not enough. Being available to friends only on our own terms does not express the kind of care about which Paul spoke. Collecting money for famine victims in Africa but remaining silent about the unjust political structures that foster oppression and starvation over the world certainly does not satisfy the obligation of *merimnaō* asked of the serious Christian.

The word implies strong feeling, a vigorous response. Christian caring, in its deepest sense, demands involvement and commitment. It is an affective movement toward another that is both honest and reverent. It is not only toward another, it is *for* the other. Caring in a biblical sense, whether expressed by a quiet concern, a gentle reaching out, or a powerful and painful anxiety about the well-being of another, never leaves us unmoved. To care is to feel. Caring does not always feel *good*. It evokes the full range of emotions—some pleasant, some unpleasant and even agonizing.

For Jesus, caring for the seventy-two who came back from their first missionary journey brought excitement and the taste of success. Caring for the multitudes, the sheep without shepherds who had oozing sores and frenzied behavior, brought weariness and often sadness. Caring for Mary of Magdala brought criticism and gossip about his judgments. Caring for Nicodemus brought frustration. Caring for Lazarus, Martha and Mary of Bethany brought friendship. Caring for the disciples as they shared a final meal brought tender expressions of transcending love. Caring en route to Calvary brought stark terror.

Many Ways to Care

For the early Christians this costly caring was profoundly inter-twined with following Jesus. It was defined in many different ways. In addition to *merimnaō*, the kind of care that could legitimately call Christians to preoccupying concern, there were other words that articulated the caring behavior of Christians in relationship to one another. The numerous expressions for human caring suggest that it was a very important dimension of discipleship.

In the first letter to the Thessalonians, caring is likened to a mother providing for her children:

> Like a mother feeding and looking after her own children,
> we felt so devoted and protective towards you, and had
> come to love you so much, that we were eager to hand
> over to you not only the Good News but our whole lives as
> well (1 Thes 2:7-8).

The expression "feeding and looking after" is also translated "taking care of" (*RSV*). It comes from the Greek *thalpō*. The word literally means "to cherish" or "to be warm toward" another. It suggests the tender devotion characteristic of a mother's love. It seeks to protect and to be near. As Paul uses the word, he refers to an immense desire to provide for the total welfare of the Thessalonians and to be united to them in personal presence.

The Greek *homeiromai* means to have affectionate desire for some-one, "to love so much." Feeling affection for another and wanting to provide care for that person often go together in relationships, as they do here for Paul.

The Tender Side of a Tough Apostle

The community of Christians at Thessalonica had special appeal for Paul. This appeal was due in part to the fact that these Christians were among his first converts and had received his message with unique enthusiasm. They were also remaining faithful to Christian teaching during persecution. Paul naturally felt pride and admiration toward them for their commitment under difficult circumstances. He also felt no small relief that his missionary efforts were showing some success.

The whole tone of Paul's letter to the Thessalonians, however, suggests more than distant admiration for a job well done. Paul evidently had strong feeling for the Thessalonians. His letter to them is filled with unrestrained expressions of affectionate caring:

> A short time after we had been separated from you—in body but never in thought . . . we had an especially strong desire and longing to see you face to face again, and we tried hard to come and visit you (Thes 2:17-18).

Paul wanted to be assured that the Thessalonians were remaining steadfast, but he also missed them in a most human way. During the time he spent with them, he became involved. He developed relationships. He experienced a presence with them that involved deep feelings and lasting ties. He grew to cherish them, to experience a mutual warmth. He cared. It lasted.

Paul not only felt care and concern for the communities himself, but he also rejoiced when he saw evidence of caring among his brothers and sisters:

> I thank God for putting into Titus' heart the same concern for you that I have myself. He did what we asked him; indeed he is more concerned than ever, and is visiting you on his own initiative (2 Cor 8:16-17).

The Greek *spoudē* means "earnest care" or, as translated above, a compelling "concern," one that moves a person to act with haste or speed. It expresses a kind of caring that urges an individual to think about another with such intensity that the other is constantly in mind. Paul was convinced that God was the source of this kind of energized caring. It was God who filled Titus' heart with feeling for the Corinthians. It was God who propelled that earnest care toward a desire for personal presence.

True to his own emotional intensity, and to his conviction that Christianity called its followers to care deeply for one another, Paul gratefully *received care* from others. He too had needs for nurturance, both physical and emotional, and he did not hesitate to express these needs or to welcome expressions of care shown toward him from others. When Paul received word from Titus that the Christians at Corinth cared about him he responded:

He [Titus] has told us all about how you want to see me,
how sorry you were, and how concerned for me, and so I
am happier now than I was before (2 Cor 7:7).

Care: To Churn From the Bowels

Luke, like Paul, was particularly concerned about the manner in
which Christians provided care for those in the community. He identified the true follower of Jesus as a caring person, as one who took risks
and incurred cost in attending to others:

But the Samaritan traveller who came upon him was
moved with compassion when he saw him. He went up
and bandaged his wounds, pouring oil and wine on them.
He then lifted him on to his own mount, carried him to
the inn and looked after him (Lk 10:33-34).

"Looked after" translates the Greek word *epimeleomai*. It is another of the words used in the writings of the Christians to describe caring behavior. It means to give attention to another. Again, the attention
given is not an impersonal regard or an obligatory observation. The
Samaritan in Luke's story "was moved with compasion." The Greek
splagchnizomai implies much more than is conveyed by the English
word "compassion." It refers to a powerful movement from within that
wells up with energy. It literally means "to churn from the bowels." The
Samaritan in the story was overcome with powerful feelings of pity for
the beaten man. Everything within him stirred up with such force that
he could scarcely contain it. The energy and feeling moved him to extend care to the helpless victim—a care that involved a most personal attentiveness.

Christian caring comes from feeling. It might excite us or drain us.
It might warm us or scare us. But it never leaves us cold. When providing service for others becomes mechanical or routine, it is technology,
not care, that is being offered. When it is extended without feeling, it
provides very little more than that which would be provided by well-
oiled machinery.

God's Care: The Source of Our Care

Luke identifies the call to care for others as having its beginnings in
Yahweh's care of the Israelites. Even though the people are wicked and
unfaithful, God never abandons them:

> And for about forty years [God] *took care of them in the*
> *wilderness* (Acts 13:18).

In caring for the Israelites, Yahweh brought them nourishment and led them out of exile. The people experienced famines and floods, wars and captivities, disappointments and losses. Throughout all of their sacred history they remembered their God as one who cared. Yahweh was the nurturing presence who sustained their lives and enabled them to experience that they were loved—even when they didn't deserve it or merit it.

At another time, and in another wilderness, that same nurturing presence was extended to Jesus:

> Then the devil left him, and angels appeared and looked
> after him (Mt 4:11).

Matthew, with his own unique fondness for heavenly messengers, indicates that the caring God of the Hebrews is still there. The Spirit, the hovering breath of God who had led Jesus into the wilderness, did not abandon him. As with the Hebrews on their journeys, God shared breath with the wandering prophet from Galilee.

Aware that God's continuous care extends beyond Jesus to all people, the author of First Peter invites Christians to "Cast all your anxieties on him [God], for he cares about you" (1 Pt 5:7-8, *RSV*). All peoples, and indeed all of creation, are of concern to God. All cause God to well up with compassion and to be moved to reach into the wilderness and ditches of human life and extend care.

A God of visiting and nourishing. A God who strains toward humanity with gentle care. A mother God who protects. A father God who feeds. A brother God who embraced our flesh, who walked with us, felt with us, and couldn't bear to leave. A spirit God who puts fire in our hearts and words on our tongues so that we might care for each other.

He Had Compassion

The early Christians found a model for human caring in Jesus. Much of his active ministry was concerned with the behaviors associated with caring. Jesus extended his care to people, and in particular to the oppressed people who had no one to look after them. But the caring attitude of Jesus was so pervasive, so much a part of his total personality, that it touched all of creation. The evangelists remembered him as one who evidenced a reverent care toward all of the earth:

> "I am the good shepherd;
> I know my own
> and my own know me, . . .
> and I lay down my life for my sheep" (Jn 10:14-15).

> "Think of the flowers growing in the fields; they never have to work or spin; . . . if that is how God clothes the grass in the field . . . will he not much more look after you?" (Mt 6:28-30).

Jesus had scanned the hillsides and watched the movements of nature. He had seen shepherds caring for their sheep, searching for them if they strayed, calling to them with a sound so familiar that the animals could recognize the voice of their own shepherd. He had seen oxen rescued from pits on the Sabbath. He had studied the horizon and noticed plump birds chirping with satisfaction. His eyes had been dazzled often by the brightly flowered fields and the multicolored meadows of his homeland.

Everything he saw in the world of nature spoke to him of a caring God who fed birds and painted flowers. He used the animals and the plants as examples of God's care—a care that was only a fraction of God's care for people.

For Jesus, caring for others was by far more important than the Sabbath observance. It broke the barriers of race and religion. It was greater than the Law itself because enabling expression of human love was the foundation and purpose of the Law in the first place. Nothing could obviate the need to care for others and no religious responsibilities could replace or excuse one from the Christian obligation to care: Not sacrifice. Not fasting. Not prayer.

Jesus expressed his care for people in all of the familiar ways. He spent time with them, time with the needy throngs and time with his closest friends. He went to dinner parties, had late night conversations, and took walks in cornfields. He shared his vision and his dreams, often pouring out his heart, to those who would listen. He established ties. He took special notice of the uncared for masses and moved out to them with forgiveness and healing time and time again:

He went about doing good and
healing (Acts 10:38, *RSV*).

He had compassion on them, and healed
their sick (Mt 14:14, *RSV*).

"My son, your sins are
forgiven" (Mk 2:5, *RSV*).

"Take heart, . . . your sins are
forgiven" (Mt 9:2, *RSV*).

It was a reverent Messiah who mingled with the bleeding, crippled
crowds. His language was filled with compassion. He never blamed
them or accused them. He stood before them with bowel-deep feeling.
Their oozing sores did not seem to repel him. Their frenzied behavior
did not frighten him. Their demands did not immobilize him. Their in-
gratitude did not make him stop.

Frequently Jesus touched those who came to him for healing:

Jesus stretched out his hand, touched him (Mt 8:3).

He touched her hand and the fever left her (Mt 8:15).

He...put his fingers into the man's ears and touched his tongue
with spittle (Mk 7:33-34).

People even brought little children to him, for him to touch them
(Lk 18:15).

He held and touched them. He argued with them, taught them,
wept over them. The involvement of Jesus with people and the expansiveness of his connectedness with them stayed fresh in the minds of the
disciples. He had been the one for others in such a complete way. He
had pushed human caring to its limits and beyond, and it had cost him
dearly. The earliest Christians remembered. They knew they could keep
his memory alive by taking the same risks for each other that he had
taken for them.

Caring and Human Integration

Christianity has always stressed the behaviors associated with human caring: affirming, healing, encouraging, forgiving, serving. These
same behaviors are those that psychologists regard as essential to good

interpersonal relationships and basic to effective communication. Human relations experts often identify the ability to care for others as an important dimension of psychological health.[18]

From a psychological perspective, caring for others means seeing their worth and letting them matter in our life. It means having the kind of respect for people that calls forth some kind of response. As in the biblical literature, psychological literature identifies different degrees and kinds of caring—and uses different words to describe caring behaviors. Whatever the word used or the degree of intensity of response, caring for others implies feeling. It is always personal.

To care for someone suggests that we have a particular way of seeing that person, an inner attitude that is basically *for* that individual. We behave toward the other with fundamental respect; we suspend all judgments. We are open to the person's self-revelations. We avoid being manipulative. Our behavior is based not on our own needs but on a keen awareness of the needs of the other.

Human caring is expressed in a variety of ways depending upon the characteristics of the relationship. Typical expressions include warmth, regard for the other's self-determination, supportive feedback, presence and behavioral gestures that communicate receptivity. Physical touch, used frequently in the gospel stories of caring, often expresses the concern associated with genuine care.

Today the word *care* refers usually to two broad categories of response: caring in order to be helpful, and caring in the sense of being involved in intimacy.

If the first instance, we are concerned for the individual. We care for the person by providing something that is needed. Our caring is like that of the Good Samaritan of the gospel toward the man in the ditch. It is primarily altruistic. It is service-oriented. It is for the other more than it is for us. We do experience some degree of feeling involvement with and toward the other which nudges us to make a choice for the other's welfare, but the care that we express is not generally indicative of a lasting relationship with the person.

In the second instance, we are fond of the individual. We care in a much more affectional sense. Our caring is less focused on helping and more focused on companionship. The feeling component of this kind of caring is usually strong and often progresses in intensity. Caring for the other is as beneficial to us as it is to the person. Like Paul's care for his Thessalonian friends, it creates a powerful desire in us to be physically present and to long for the other from our depths.

The Extremes of Caring

There is a fine line between caring and controlling. Sustaining and smothering are not the same thing. Sometimes, in our eagerness to please, to ease our own floundering security, or to meet our own needs to be needed, we can lose perspective on the real meaning of healthy nurturing and Christian caring. Such may be the case with an over-protective parent, a jealous friend, or a dominating lover.

A truly caring person has discovered the middle ground of genuine caring amid its extremes of coldness and control. Others experience freedom in the presence of such a person. They are able to be agents in their own lives and not captives imprisoned in the web of possessiveness. They feel cared for without feeling governed, reverenced but not worshipped. They know they are cherished without being owned.

There are some individuals who carry concern for others to such an extreme that they appear more doting than caring. They are consistently waiting in the wings, ever anxious to help whether help is needed or not. The behaviors of some of these people are common enough to form a kind of pattern called the *doter syndrome*. Certain distinguishing characteristics make them easy to spot. They *always* hold the door for others and exit last. They *always* sit in the back seat. They *always* stand at the end of the line. They prepare a meal but don't eat it themselves until it's cold because they are so busy jumping up and down to cut more roast or pour more coffee. Theirs is a "ready or not here I come" attitude; they are forever fetching things, waiting on people, and meeting everyone else's needs, often at the serious expense of their own. They are usually ill-at-ease unless they are functioning in the waiter's role. Being a guest, and being served by someone else, is painful for them.

While this pseudo-caring is seen in both women and men, it tends to be more common in women, particularly the housewife who has learned that her primary role in life is to take care of others and the Catholic nun who has been taught to minimize her own needs in the interest of service and self-denial.

Usually people who feel compelled to wait on others are insecure and lack a strong sense of self-worth. They also seem to lack an ability to perceive how their behavior affects others. The only way available for them to feel good about themselves is to wait on others, even if those others do not seem to welcome their service.

Years of self-negating service take their toll eventually. A high degree of repressed anger, depression, and numerous physical symptoms are common to such individuals, particularly after middle age. People who are so oriented toward helping others that they fail to care for themselves do not do well in relationships. They tend to irritate others and drive them away with their over-solicitous ways.

Genuine caring does not overwhelm people. It does not cause them to feel intruded upon. It does not create a hustle-and-bustle atmosphere. It does not promote helplessness. It does not negate the self.

Genuine caring is attuned to the response of the person or persons being cared for in a situation. It senses when to move closer and when to back off. It does not rush in to do for others what they can or ought to do for themselves.

While the extremes of caring for others such as doting or controlling are often seen in relationships, the opposite is also common. To be care-less or without care literally means to be idle in response to another. Being uncaring means feeling nothing or doing nothing in relationship to others. Uncaring people have no emotional movement toward people. There is distance in their eyes and coldness in their hearts. Their presence warms no one.

People who cannot care for others are often those who have not experienced being cared for in their own personal lives. Perhaps they were neglected as children or hurt in relationships. They have learned that caring is painful and have decided that it is not worth it. Instead of moving toward others, they move away from them in an act of self-protection. They might appear shy or withdrawn; they might act harsh or aggressive. They might use humor or alcohol or work to keep people at a distance emotionally. Whatever psychological mechanism they use to wall in their own feelings, and to wall out the feelings of others, theirs is a lonely world. They are often as emotionally idle in response to themselves as they are toward others. Though they hunger for nourishment and ache for the warmth of human closeness, their consciousness of these needs has been dulled into oblivion. Because they have no real care for themselves that is not tinged with self-protection, they have difficulty caring for others.

At Once She Straightened Up

Caring for others—making a move toward them that is touched by reverence and charged with feeling—is as Christian as it is healthy. Without it, a person cannot claim to be integrated—whole. Without it, an individual cannot claim to be faithful to the gospel—holy.

Genuine caring changes people. It enables growth. It creates a base of strength. It invites people to find their way home to their own truth. In the scriptural accounts of Jesus' life and ministry it can be seen that the style of his caring always empowered people. His contacts and interactions with people resulted in their growth. They became stronger, more faithful, able to stand on their own, able to arrive at new understandings:

> She was bent double and quite unable to stand upright. When Jesus saw her he called her over and said, "Woman, you are rid of your infirmity" and he laid his hands on her. And at once she straightened up, and she glorified God (Lk 13:11-13).

> The woman put down her water jar and hurried back to the town to tell the people, "Come and see a man who has told me everything I ever did; I wonder if he is the Christ?" . . . Many Samaritans of that town had believed in him on the strength of the woman's testimony (Jn 4:28-29, 39).

To care for people is to enable them to stand upright. It is to take away the obstacles that weigh them down and keep them helpless. It is to relate to them face to face, eye to eye. To talk with them as equals. To touch them with truth and fill them with a sense of worth that spills over into other relationships. It is to stand aside and let them have their glory.

Warm people. Concerned people. Affectionate people. Feeling for others. Moving toward them. Nourishing hearts and sustaining lives with their very presence. These are the people who speak to us about discipleship and tell us that Christianity is real. They care. They remind us of a God who cares.

7

THE WORD BECAME FLESH

The Biblical Significance of Words

The Word was made flesh
he lived among us,
and we saw his glory,
the glory that is his as the only Son of the Father,
full of grace and truth (Jn 1:14).

Throughout the Hebrew and Christian scriptures, the word of God has awesome power. God's word effects creation, sustains the Israelites through their wanderings, and puts fire in the hearts of the prophets. It is dynamic and faithful. It becomes flesh. It enters into intimate communication with men and women.

Communication is many-faceted. It has to do with expressions and gestures, with symbols and words, with feelings and actions, with minds and with flesh. We have been looking at communication in some of its less verbal dimensions: listening, attending to feelings, caring. While each of these areas is essential to the total communication process, the important vehicle of words cannot be minimized. Words provide a vital link between inner experience and outward clarification of that experience. Human closeness and its meaningful expression depend on words and how they are used. The timing, choice and tone of words can often make the difference between conflict or enjoyment in human interaction.

Listening enables a person to know something of another's world. Being aware of feelings is related to a healthy self-knowledge. Having

111

genuine care for others is important to developing and maintaining relationships.

But we can listen and not respond to what we have heard. We can be aware of our feelings and hide them. We can care and not tell anyone. Gestures and other non-verbal symbols can help us express some of our thoughts, feelings, and experiences some of the time, but they can never be complete substitutes for words.

We need words. We are a people fashioned and fed by the word of a nourishing God. We are born out of covenants and promises that have been expressed in words and spoken with courage for thousands of years. Our memories burn with words carved on stone tablets and written on scrolls. We are the people of Jesus, Word of God, who spoke words that we might live.

Because the ancient peoples attributed such significance to the word, the human word as well as God's word, a closer look at its meaning in biblical times can add depth to our exploration of human communication.

Our Word Does Not Return to Us Empty

In the world of the Hebrews, word (*dãbãr*) and its corresponding reality were completely identified with each other. To speak a word, particularly speaking with solemnity, was automatically to effect what was spoken. To speak a word was also to reveal something of a person's identity. The very self was contained in an individual's word. To speak a word was to release energy—a powerful, personal force that could not be called back.

An example of the effective force of words occurs in the Pentateuch when Isaac gives his blessing to Jacob instead of to Esau. Even though Isaac didn't intend the blessing for Jacob, once his words were spoken, the blessing was effected. He couldn't "take it back." Even though his words of blessing were a mistake, they had power, and that power had long-term consequences.

If human words effected what was spoken, this was even more true of the word of God:

> Yes, as the rain and the snow come down from the heavens
> and do not return without watering the earth, making it
> yield and giving growth to provide seed for the sower and

> bread for the eating, so the word that goes from my
> mouth does not return to me empty, without carrying out
> my will and succeeding in what it was sent to do (Is
> 55:10-11).

Isaiah was not talking about words that predicted the future or manipulated human history. Rather, the prophet was expressing the belief
that God's words can be counted upon to accomplish the reality that
they express. Like the rains and snow, God's word yields something. It
has a purpose and a mission, and it is active until it has accomplished its
purpose and fulfilled its mission. God sees to that:

> Then Yahweh said, "Well seen! I too watch over my word
> to see it fulfilled" (Jer 1:12).

God's Words in the Prophet's Mouth

That powerful, purposeful, promising word is shared with human
beings. Jeremiah receives God's word into his mouth and experiences an
electrifying force that takes over his whole being:

> Then Yahweh put out his hand and touched my mouth
> and said to me:
> "There! I am putting my words into your mouth"
> (Jer 1:9).

> The word of Yahweh has meant for me
> insult, derision, all day long.
> I used to say, "I will not think about him,
> I will not speak in his name any more."
> Then there seemed to be a fire burning in my heart,
> imprisoned in my bones.
> The effort to restrain it wearied me
> I could not bear it (Jer 20:8-9).

The word of God came to Jeremiah with such consuming power
that it could not be contained or resisted. The word had a destiny that
became fused with Jeremiah's own destiny. It wielded such force that it
controlled Jeremiah, even against his desire.

When Ezekiel ate the scroll on which was written the word of Yahweh, he too was touched by the consequence of having taken in God's
word:

113

> I opened my mouth; he gave me the scroll to eat and said,
> "Son of man, feed and be satisfied by the scroll I am giv-
> ing you." I ate it, and it tasted sweet as honey (Ez 3:2-3).

No one who experiences God's word is left unaffected. That word
can weary or it can warm, but it never lies unnoticed. "The personality
of the prophet is invaded through the word by the personality of Yahweh."[19] The fire of Yahweh becomes the fire of the prophet. The unrestrainable energy of God becomes the unrestrainable energy of the person to whom God speaks. The voice of the prophet who consumes God's
word is now the voice of God.

According to the biblical mentality, words enter a person—they get
inside. There they are alive with a powerful energy that enables something of the speaker to penetrate, to enter another's core. It is in the
shared word that the speaker and the one spoken to make contact. It is
there that they meet each other. It is there that their destinies become
intwined, and they are one.

The Urgency of Words

Though focus is often on the word as it applies to the word of God
in the Hebrew scriptures, the wisdom literature recognizes that human
words, too, have power and influence. The psalmist experiences this and
is almost overcome by the pressure of words bursting to be spoken:

> I said, "I will watch how I behave,
> and not let my tongue lead me into sin;
> I will keep a muzzle on my mouth
> as long as the wicked man is near me."
> I stayed dumb, silent, speechless,
> though the sight of him thriving made torment increase.
>
> My heart had been smouldering inside me,
> but it flared up at the thought of this
> and the words burst out (Ps 39:1-3).

Like the fire inside Jeremiah, like the overwhelming compulsion experienced by anyone straining to contain words that are uncontainable,
the words inside the psalmist shatter all resistance. The psalmist's experience is a familiar one: Words that smolder. Words that flare up. Words

that burst out even when we are struggling to keep them in. Words seem to have the same power today. They sometimes seem to have a life and will of their own, independent from the speaker. Theirs can be a power so strong, a force so great that the speaker feels helpless before them.

It is precisely the awareness of the power of words that urged the wisdom writers to comment repeatedly on the way words are employed in human interaction. Even though words have a propulsion of their own and the urgency of words is hard to resist, the speaker still has a responsibility for the words fashioned in his or her heart.

Words can "soothe more than oil" (Ps 55:21) or be as fierce as "fire" in your mouth (Jer 5:14). They can be appropriate and "aptly spoken" (Prv 25:11) or out of place and rambling, a "flood of words" (Prv 10:19). Words can deceive and be "snares" (Prv 12:6) and words can be "truthful" (Eccl 12:10). They wound (Prv 18:8) and they heal (Ps 107:20). Whether words do violence or nourish, they come out of the depth of a person's being.

It was a common belief in biblical times that those of wicked hearts could only utter words of wickedness, while those of integrity brought forth words of goodness. Evil people thus effected evil deeds through their words. Good people could not help but effect goodness, since goodness was the condition of the heart which gave birth to the words.

Words, then, while they sometimes seemed to have a power of their own, still were connected to the speaker in some way. They were dependent upon the speaker for their identity and character, for their goodness or badness, for their honesty or their corruption. Words lived in hearts. Hearts gave shape to words. While those words swelled with independent power, they could not be disconnected from the heart. The same is true today.

The Word As Good News

In the Christian scriptures, *word* is most often used with reference to the gospel, or to the word of God. It is a continuation of the word spoken through the prophets. Now, it has found a home in the person of Jesus. It has become the good news. It has been made flesh—more intimate, more urgent, more deeply connected to humanity.

As good news, God's word still has the same dynamism and power reminiscent of the Hebrew scriptures. From the earliest Christian writings, the word of God is alive with personality and power.

> When we brought the Good News to you, it came to you
> not only as words, but as power and as the Holy Spirit and
> as utter conviction (1 Thes 1:5).

That earliest word resounds with life. It lives (1 Thes 2:13). It spreads (2 Thes 3:1). It reconciles (2 Cor 5:19). It consumes the whole life of the one in whom it dwells (1 Thes 2:8-9).

The Word Takes Flesh

In the Johannine writings the meaning of *the word* takes on a new and different emphasis. In John, the word is not the gospel, but the person of Jesus. The word of God is no longer the word spoken through the prophet. The word is the prophet. And the prophet is the word.

The word of old that lit up the night and spun forth stars too numerous to count, the word that propelled breath into creatures and quickened them with life, the word that seared the hearts of the patriarchs and thundered from mountain tops—that word could no longer contain itself in prophets and stars.

With all of the power of earlier utterances, God's uncontainable word bounded out of itself in a final act of self-transcendence. Longing for union and restless for love, God's own self-expression became human. A word too profound for prophets and too urgent to hold back—a word too personal for law and too fleshy for the heavens—it became incarnate.

This incarnate word was no longer a message to deliver but a person to know, a person like us, a person of flesh. A baby who gurgled and burped. A child who ran in the wind. A youth filled with ideas and flooded with feelings. A blue-collar worker with calloused hands. A neighbor who slept and ate, laughed and cried, fished and visited. A friend whose arms knew how to hug, whose genitals felt desire, whose heart yearned for love. A person like us.

Jesus the Word

This word-person, Jesus, lived in a world of words. He knew the words of the prophets before him. He had memorized words written on scrolls. He wrestled with the words of the Law. He was nourished by every word that came from the mouth of God. He was angered by the crooked words of hypocrites and moved by the pitiful words of the op-

116

pressed. He restored words to the mouths of the dumb. He used words that awed some and scared others. He taught with forceful words and died with words of surrender on his lips.

Jesus experienced the gamut of human speech. He knew that words had power. He knew that words could heal the heart or betray it. Jesus needed words. He asked others to give him their words—words of loyalty, words of faith, words of friendship. And, in turn, he shared his words with them.

We know something about the impact that the words of Jesus have had on human history, yet we know very little about his actual verbal style. He left no verbatims. We do not have a single word penned from his own hand. His words were not recorded for 20 or more years after his death. And then, they were written by individuals who had not actually known him, and who were writing in a world heavily influenced by patriarchy, Greco-Roman culture, and the secular philosophies of the day.

Scripture scholars agree that the sayings of Jesus which probably come the closest to his actual words include:

— the sayings about the kingdom[20]

— the Lord's prayer

— the proverbial sayings

— the parables

It is from these sayings that we can glean the most accurate picture of his verbal style. While the actual formulation of the words and sayings of Jesus comes from the evangelists, the content, at least in the four categories listed above, echoes the voice of Jesus and is reminiscent of Jesus' own style of talking.

Schüssler-Fiorenza has recently focused a new emphasis on the authority of New Testament words and sayings. Because Christian faith hinges on belief in a kingdom characterized by equality and freedom from oppression, Schüssler-Fiorenza suggests that only those scriptural words which break through the barrier of patriarchal oppression and support the liberation of all people can claim the theological authority of revelation.[21] This further suggests that the words and sayings found on the lips of Jesus can be considered part of revelation only if they are experienced as liberating for all people and consistent with his vision of a discipleship of equals. Any sayings experienced as oppressive, or used to support the oppression of any group, cannot be considered authentic, but rather, a result of the influence of the times.

Following the Word

Where does all of this leave us with regard to better understanding human communication, a communication that is at once psychologically healthy and compatible with Christian discipleship?

We are called to follow Jesus of Nazareth, to model our lives after his. Part of living is talking. Is there a characteristically Christian way of talking? Is it possible to learn something about how we should use words when the words of the one we follow are so elusive?

Following does not mean copying. Following does not mean parroting another's verbal style. Following does not mean duplicating someone else's personality. Biblical following means walking alongside Jesus of Nazareth, in the context of his own time in history, and being profoundly influenced by him—all the while retaining our own identity and personality.

To communicate as Jesus communicated, to enflesh his message, means staying near enough to his words to be influenced by them, yet far enough away to have perspective on how they can speak to our times.

We cannot know exactly how Jesus spoke or exactly what he said. That is not important to following. What we do know is that he was filled with an all-consuming zeal for the reign of God—a freeing, liberating kingdom where human beings valued each other's dignity as sons and daughters of God. We know that he spoke of that kingdom with words that were so urgent, so disquieting, so compelling, that they have been remembered for nearly two thousand years. We know the memories of those whose lives were touched and changed by hearing him speak. Let us look at some of those memories.

The Words of Jesus

The first evangelists preached the message of Jesus as clearly and forcefully as they knew how. They trusted the Spirit to cause the simple kerygma to take root and grow in the hearts of the early Christians. Perhaps they drew their initial simplicity and straightforward clarity from their memories of Jesus, from recollections of the man who walked in their midst and spoke his truth without grandiose words, and without fear of the consequences of his honesty.

The Kingdom Sayings

All of the evangelists remembered Jesus as a proclaimer—as one whose words called attention not to himself but to the kingdom of God. The proclamation of the kingdom occupied Jesus from dawn until dusk throughout his public ministry. It was with crisp clarity that he signaled the nearness of that kingdom:

"The time has come" he said "and the kingdom of God is close at hand" (Mk 1:15).

"The kingdom of God is not coming with signs to be observed; nor will they say, 'Lo, here it is!' or 'There!' for behold, the kingdom of God is in the midst of you (Lk 17:20-21, RSV).

There are over one hundred kingdom sayings on the lips of Jesus in the gospels. Most are considered authentic. From sheer numbers it is easy to see that the proclamation of the kingdom was of paramount importance to Jesus.

There are two clear characteristics of the kingdom that emerge from all of these sayings: It is now. It is inclusive. It is "bursting into human life in unsuspecting ways among apparently undeserving people."[22]

Proverbial Sayings

The proverbial sayings offer us another medium in which to draw near to the words of Jesus and to feel something of his authentic message. Proverbs state the obvious. They presuppose that the speaker has looked around, has made some observations, and wishes to comment on them. Apparently Jesus had been observant. He had listened to the earth on which he walked and to the people it carried. He saw prophets being rejected among their own. He saw the overly satisfied trying to experience the inclusive love of the kingdom, and finding it difficult to let go of the abundance that kept them separated from their brothers and sisters. He saw households turned against each other. He saw the oppressed being abused. He wanted to comment on his observations; he wanted to seize another opportunity to present his vision:

"A prophet is only despised in his own country, among his own relations and in his own house" (Mk 6:4).

"How hard it is for those who have riches to enter the
kingdom of God!" (Mk 10:23).

"And if a household is divided against itself, that household can never stand" (Mk 3:25).

"Love your enemies and pray for those who persecute
you" (Mt 5:44).

Jesus does not use words to gain popularity with anyone. He does
not say what people want to hear in order to please them. His solid convictions press him to be candid. At the same time, he is not brutal; his
vision shuts out no one. Compassion is woven through his words. He
feels the loneliness of the rejected prophet. He understands the frailty of
those who live divided lives. He is honest with the rich but not condemning. He believes that the oppressed are capable of radical love.

The Prayer Jesus Taught

Jesus' words at prayer are as faithful to his vision as are his words to
the crowds. He sees a situation in which the values of the kingdom will
be held central, where all people will have bread, where reconciliation
will be foundational to relationships:

"Father, may your name be held holy,
your kingdom come;
give us each day our daily bread,
and forgive us our sins,
for we ourselves forgive each one who is in debt to us.
And do not put us to the test" (Lk 11:2-4).

With the crowds, Jesus is sincere and real. He comes before God
the same way. He longs for the coming of the kingdom, and so he prays.
He asks us to pray the same way.

The Parables

The parabolic sayings give us a final look at the authentic words of
Jesus. In the parables Jesus frames his message not in a single, pithy
statement but in a story. Jewish rabbis used parables, so the crowds
around Jesus would have been accustomed to this method of teaching.
In a parable a familiar thing (fine pearls) is compared to a less familiar
thing (kingdom) so that its meaning can be carried over.[23] Jesus used
parables in talking about the kingdom to make it more familiar.

Much of what Jesus had to say involved a radical shift in belief for his hearers. Framing the message in a parable called attention to that shift.[24] The parable of the Good Samaritan illustrates this. The Jews of Jesus' day despised the Samaritans. When Jesus tells a story combining "good" and "Samaritan," he is asking his hearers to imagine the unimaginable—that Samaritans could possibly be good and capable of compassionate action. The straightforward style, the progressive story line, the detailed description of the Samaritan's kindness, all would have commanded the attention and evoked a response in any righteous Jew of the day.

When Jesus had a conviction, when longing for the kingdom surged inside of him, he could not hold back his urgent need to present his vision to all who would listen. Whether he uttered a proverb, spoke in parables, prayed, or described the coming of God's kingdom in some other way, his words were focused on the same central message: The experience of God is now and it is characterized by the presence of inclusive love.

Words That Express the Vision

We began this reflection on the words of Jesus with these questions: Is there a characteristically Christian way of talking? Is it possible to learn something about how we should use words when the words of the one we follow are so elusive?

While the exact words and phrases spoken by the historical Jesus remain shrouded in the past, the content of those words certainly clusters around one central theme: A kingdom characterized by inclusive love.

Most of what Jesus actually verbalized concerned some dimension of that vision: Where people would find it. How they would become part of it. Who would be in it. And who would not. Jesus preached a discipleship which did not exclude people, but rather, pulled them into the center where all were equal. Those invited to the "head table" were precisely those who were left out in the real world of religion, politics and society: the poor, the sinners, the outcasts, the women. In the expansiveness of the kingdom, people would no longer be divided and assigned separate roles according to economics, sex or righteousness. Rather, all would be equal: rich and poor, sinners and righteous, women and men, sick and well.

If we use the kingdom vision as a model for our own verbal style, the implications are obvious: Our choice of words must be faithful to

121

the discipleship of equals which Jesus proclaimed. Following Jesus means using language that recognizes all people. Using words which shut some people out, which insult them as a group, or which promote or suggest inequality simply does not fit with following Jesus of Nazareth.

In our own time there has been much discussion and much disagreement about the need to use inclusive language in the liturgy and in the formal prayer of the community. If the liturgy is supposed to be an expression of the kingdom vision of Jesus, the gathering of his followers around the festive table, then it is unthinkable that the words used at such a gathering would not be fully expressive of the values of inclusive love for which that vision stands.

If the vehicles of human communication—the words we use to talk to one another—need any single characteristic in order to be considered Christian, it is the characteristic of inclusive love. Our choice of words must point toward the reality in which we believe, and the vision of the one we say we follow.

Words which ridicule others, ignore them, insult them, abuse them, and exclude them are not Christian. They do not promote communication that is holy. Racial slurs, denigrating terms for the poor and sexist language have no place among those who claim to be Christian.

Reactions to the Words of Inclusive Love

The evangelists all emphasize that people had mixed reactions to Jesus, but they did react. Jesus attracted both friends and enemies because of his words:

> And he won the approval of all, and they were astonished by the gracious words that came from his lips (Lk 4:22).

> And his teaching made a deep impression on them because he spoke with authority (Lk 4:32).
> These words caused disagreement among the Jews. Many said, "He is possessed, he is raving; why bother to listen to him?" Others said, "These are not the words of a man possessed by the devil: could a devil open the eyes of the blind?" (Jn 10:19-21)

Some of the people who encountered the message of inclusive love said of its proclaimer, "He is a good man" (Jn 7:12). Others who heard the same message said of Jesus, "No, he is leading the people astray" (Jn 7:12). Some who heard about the discipleship of equals marveled and came to believe in him. Others who heard about it were indignant and wanted him out of the way. It appears that the same is true today.

Inviting people to live in a reality characterized by inclusiveness and equality evokes strong responses in people. Everyone reacted to Jesus. They felt something in response to his message. A hearer could dislike it, disbelieve it, distort it, be discomforted by it. But no one who stood before Jesus of Nazareth, no one who experienced his far-reaching love for the people at the fringes, could claim to be unaffected.

Jesus went on talking no matter what the response. The truth of his wild and earthy vision burned within him. He could not hold it back. He had to give it flesh:

> The Word was made flesh
> he lived among us,
> and we saw his glory,
> the glory that is his as the only Son of the Father,
> full of grace and truth (Jn 1:14).

Like the Word we follow, our words must become flesh. They must be inviting, inclusive and loving, expressing the glory that is ours as the people of God, full of grace and truth.

8

IF YOU MAKE MY WORD YOUR HOME

Words in Relationships

To the Jews who believed in him Jesus said:

"If you make my word your home
you will indeed be my disciples,
you will learn the truth
and the truth will make you free" (Jn 8:31-32).

In the previous chapter we looked at the biblical meaning of *word* and at the authentic words of Jesus as they have been handed on to us in the writings of the evangelists. In this chapter we will examine the implications of that word for relationships.

In John's gospel, Jesus makes it clear that part of discipleship involves making "my word your home." It requires moving in with the word of Jesus, living with it, and growing progressively more one with the expansive vision that the word articulates.

Receptivity to the Word

The fact that many people heard the word of Jesus and could not be at home with it illustrates the terrible vulnerability of a word that has been shared: It can be so easily dismissed and so angrily rejected. It can be refused a home. An idea as wonderful as a kingdom where all would be brothers and sisters cannot be welcomed by those whose hearing is muffled by a personal agenda.

In Mark's gospel the Jews were struggling to understand the meaning of a crucified Messiah. They had expected a triumphant savior, a warrior-like leader who would sweep them toward political victory. When their expectations confronted the reality of the gentle Suffering Servant preaching inclusive love, many of them could not accept him. They could not reconcile words of peace with their need for war. They could not listen to words of love and equality when they had enemies to overcome. They could not receive words that challenged their assumptions and shattered their time-honored traditions. Some of them accepted Jesus initially, but their acceptance gradually turned to coldness, and finally to open hostility when his words did not fit their expectations.

The insecure, the frightened, the hostile, the self-righteous—all have difficulty with receptivity to words that do not match their needs. When emotions are volatile and expectations are threatened, words cannot be heard as they are intended.

This fact often causes a great deal of pain in relationships. Words are spoken, and someone who lacks the basic receptivity necessary to hear them accurately distorts their meaning or refuses to acknowledge their possible truth. No manner of rephrasing or dialogue seems to help.

Jesus appeared to understand the important influence of receptivity. Nowhere do the evangelists suggest that he forced his words on anyone. He is never presented as disregarding people's right to accept or reject his message. He does not use words to coerce or to intimidate. Even when others are not openly unreceptive, but simply find his words too demanding, he does not coax allegiance:

> "If you wish to be perfect, go and sell what you own and give the money to the poor, and you will have treasure in heaven; then come, follow me." But when the young man heard these words he went away sad, for he was a man of great wealth (Mt 19:21-22).

That is the end of the story. Matthew's Jesus does not go after the man with one final sales pitch. Nor does he water down his message to make it more appealing. He lets him go.

John tells a similar story. After some of his disciples become upset with his words and stop going with him, Jesus turns to the twelve and says, "What about you, do you want to go away too?" (Jn 6:67). He respects their freedom to accept or reject his vision. He does not want his words to induce false loyalty.

Finding Words That Get Through

Each of the evangelists presents Jesus as a person who took particular care to speak in a manner that would be understood by his contemporaries if they had "ears to hear." He does not want to pressure his hearers, but he does want to "get through." He wants his words to reach people's hearts and make a difference. He wants them to hear his words, and from there be able to picture the kingdom, to feel its nearness. When his words baffle the sincere, he willingly re-explains his message, further clarifying what his disciples do not yet understand:

"This is what I meant when I said" . . . He then opened
their minds to understand (Lk 24:44, 45).

Because each of the evangelists attempted to speak to a particular audience, each emphasized a unique aspect of Jesus' life and message. They took great care to portray him in a manner that would speak most effectively to the personal lives of their hearers.

One of the ways that they did this was through language. Jesus uses words, symbols, metaphors that are familiar to those he is addressing. He travelled among shepherds, fishermen, the Jewish milieu. So he talks of himself as the Good Shepherd, and as one who would teach his followers to be fishers of souls. He makes use of familiar images: foxes in their dens, birds in their nests, sowers in fields, wheat ready for the harvest. For the common people, Jesus talks of lost sheep and nets filled with fishes. For the more sophisticated leaders, he uses images of offerings and altars, tithes and tombs. Jesus is presented as one who has great verbal flexibility, a skill enabling him to adapt his verbal style to different people and different situations. Contemporary psychological research shows that people who demonstrate verbal flexibility and sensitivity to people's environment are highly effective communicators. They have maximized their chances of getting their message across.

Words Flow Out of What Fills the Heart

Whether at prayer or with people, Jesus speaks words that are congruent with his heart. He does not clutter his message with deliberately concealed meanings or unspoken expectations. He does not set people up. In fact, he deplores this kind of verbal manipulation when the Pharisees use it on him:

> Then the pharisees went away to work out between them
> how to trap him in what he said. . . . But Jesus was aware
> of their malice and replied, "You hypocrites! Why do you
> set this trap for me?" (Mt 22:15, 18).

Theirs was a classic example of a hidden agenda. Their words were calculated to hide their real intentions. They were using language to confuse rather than to clarify, behavior as common today as it was then. Jesus named their game and refused to participate in their evil verbal gymnastics.

Jesus recognized that words are extremely important in human communication. Words have power. That power can be good or bad. The manner in which people use that power says something about the state of their souls before God.

In Matthew's gospel Jesus is openly critical of those who put up polite facades and attempt to deceive and manipulate others with words that are incongruent with interior attitudes. Some of his most vehement sayings are directed toward those whose words convey one message while their actions convey another. He calls them "hypocrites" and "vipers" precisely because their behavior and their words do not fit with each other. He seems to particularly loathe this form of deceit because it is a source of confusion and oppression for people. When a person's interior and exterior words are not integrated, it becomes easier and easier to use people and exalt oneself. Jesus has a harsh message for those who abuse the gift of verbal speech. Matthew's Jesus is convinced that the kingdom of God has no room for those of wily words and dark designs:

> "Brood of vipers, how can your speech be good when you
> are evil? For a man's words flow out of what fills his
> heart. A good man draws good things from his store of
> goodness; a bad man draws bad things from his store of
> badness. So I tell you this, that for every unfounded word
> men utter they will answer on Judgement day, since it is
> by your words you will be acquitted, and by your words
> condemned" (Mt 12:34-37).

In Greek, an "unfounded word" was an "idle word." It was idle because it literally did nothing that a word should do. It did not express truth. It did not convey genuine meaning. It did not reveal the heart. Rather than clarifying the intentions of the speaker, the idle word obscured them. The idle word could be uttered because the speaker failed

128

to reflect on the implications of his or her words before speaking, or it could represent a deliberate attempt on the part of the speaker to deceive. Whether the idle word was spoken because the speaker was careless, or malicious, was not particularly important. As in Old Testament times, words had dynamic reality—consequences. Since it was within the power of the speaker to reflect before speaking and to make appropriate choices about words, that speaker had to assume responsibility for the effect of those word choices. If evil resulted from the speaker's idle words, then the speaker was responsible for the evil.

Idle words are disconnected from the heart. They have no potential for life. They serve no communicative function because they do not enable people to move toward one another. They hide rather than reveal. They darken rather than illumine.

Jesus frequently urges his disciples to be open—to operate in the light. The kingdom is not to be a place of whispers and shadows. It does not keep secrets or provide a refuge for disguises. It attracts attention. It lights up windows and shouts from rooftops. It announces. It speaks a word. It is a home for those of open speech and transparent hearts:

> Everything that is now covered will be uncovered, and everything now hidden will be made clear. For this reason, whatever you have said in the dark will be heard in the daylight, and whatever you have whispered in hidden places will be proclaimed on the housetops (Lk 12:2-3).

Say But the Word

The word of Jesus was remembered by later Christians as having tremendous power, that same power characteristic of the God of the Hebrews, that same power that effected what it spoke. It had particular power to effect healing:

> "Sir, I am not worthy to have you under my roof; just give the word and my servant will be cured." . . . And to the centurion Jesus said, "Go back, then; you have believed, so let this be done for you." And the servant was cured at that moment (Mt 8:8,13).

Jesus did not speak healing words because people had earned them or deserved them. It was precisely the unworthy and the undeserving who most often experienced restoration in response to the word of Jesus.

So often in relationships, particularly when there is brokenness, healing words are not spoken because one person feels that it is up to the other to make the first move. How often are healing words avoided because:

> "It's up to her to come to me. I went to her last time. . . ."
> "It wasn't my fault. He's going to have to apologize first.
> . . ." "I'm not going to say anything more. They don't deserve it."

Of course, it is not always possible to effect healing in relationships by being the first to reach out. Nor is it always appropriate to push for reconciliation. But in those instances where I avoid initiating it because the other is undeserving, or because it is not my turn, I am withholding words that might well have power to heal. I am like the reluctant prophet, resisting God's healing word within me because it causes me discomfort.

Those Who Hear the Word and Put It Into Practice

It is the activation of the healing word in everyday situations that differentiates the true disciple of Jesus from the outsider. For Jesus, it was not enough for his followers to simply hear the word, agree with it, and then live as they had before receiving it. Jesus was not after agreement. He wanted radical commitment and total personal change from his disciples—a change that showed itself in relationships.

Luke was careful to assure his Gentile audience that it was not the presence of Jewish blood that gave a person claim to Jesus' friendship, but rather, the presence of the lived word in a person's life. Putting this word into practice bonded Christians together in a way so profound that it created new and deeper relationships, relationships far more significant than could ever be effected by blood ties:

> He was told, "Your mother and brothers are standing outside and want to see you." But he said in answer, "My mother and my brothers are those who hear the word of God and put it into practice" (Lk 8:20-21).

Jesus seemed to understand that putting the word into practice did not happen all at once in the life of the disciple. It is particularly in

John's gospel where we learn that taking the word from our ears to our life involves a journey—a movement from hiddenness to openness, from lack of perception to full understanding.

The things Jesus did and said were signs that had a certain obvious meaning as well as a deeper meaning that the disciples would understand later. While Jesus is presented as speaking clearly and honestly, his words have a depth that his followers cannot yet understand. In the beginning they hear his words. They take the first step on the journey toward full understanding by receiving the verbal message into their hearts. But it is only later, after they have made the death-resurrection journey themselves, that his words take on new clarity. Their understanding is progressive. It begins with simple hearing. It is transformed with life experience. It culminates in deep understanding:

> But he was speaking of the sanctuary that was his body,
> and when Jesus rose from the dead, his disciples remembered that he had said this, and they believed the scripture
> and the words he had said (Jn 2:21-22).

Often, we are asked to take that same journey. We hear someone's words. We comprehend the obvious meaning. Yet there is something more, something about the message that we don't fully see. Perhaps the words deliver great pain. Perhaps they invite us into the unexpected. Perhaps they seem too good to be true or too unfair to accept. Perhaps at the time they even seem insignificant. It is only later, after we have come to know the implications of the words, that they take on clarity. Only after we have made a death-resurrection journey with the message does its meaning for our lives sink in. Our understanding is progressive. It begins with simple hearing. It is transformed with life experience. It culminates in discovering the deeper Word of our lives.

My Word Is Not My Own

Whenever the evangelists depict Jesus talking about the "word," it is never understood as Jesus' own word. Particularly in John's gospel, Jesus emphasizes that the word he speaks and the message he delivers is not his own, but God's:

> And my word is not my own:
> it is the word of the one who sent me (Jn 14:24).

Enfleshing that word in our life effects a transforming unity between the disciple and the divine. It was this word, with its power to connect the human and the divine, that drove Jesus to proclaim, to heal, to teach, and finally, to die.

The more the early Christians remembered his words and retold his stories, the more they realized that Jesus had lived his word like no one they had ever known. So faithful was Jesus to this word from God, so imbued with it, that it became his identity. His life was so true to his word that Jesus and his word seemed as one. He not only spoke the word of God. He was that word.

He lived among us, and we saw his glory. We saw that he was ablaze with a prophet's words, powerful words that jarred the complacent and liberated the oppressed. But most important, words that were always true to his heart.

Jesus faced the world with his word. His word was his way of making contact with people, of clarifying his vision, of expressing his feelings, of letting his friends know how much he loved them. He used words when he was angry. Words when he was lonely. Words when he was dying.

Jesus used words as words should be used, not to describe data but to break through the surface to the real truth of human life. That is how we are to use words—not to confuse, not to impress, not to deceive, not to attack, but to break through. We are to use words to break through insult and injury to forgiveness, to break through secretive, hidden ways to opennness, to break through silence to conversation. We are to use words as Jesus did: to heal and to liberate, and to give honest expression to the word of God within us.

The Communicative Function of Words

Most people today are aware that communication is important, and that it has something to do with listening and with expressing feelings in relationships. We know this in theory if not always in practice. However, when it comes to choosing the words and the tone of voice to adequately express the feelings, many of us fall into old habits.

We have learned to beat around the bush, to drop hints, to water down or blurt out what we want to say. Then we are hurt or offended when others don't seem to get our message. Studies show that the step from awareness of feelings to an appropriate verbal expression of them often fails because of a lack of verbal clarity:

An elderly woman tells her married son that she is planning to have a quiet weekend, and secretly hopes that he will hear her loneliness and invite her for Sunday dinner. . . . A husband assumes that his wife knows how much he loves her, even though he never says the words. . . . A college student maintains a sulky silence for days in an effort to let his roommates know that he is angry with them. . . . A young woman tells a friend how depressed she is feeling on the day her friend is leaving for vacation . . . .

Our words are often containers of hidden hopes and cloudy expectations. Our silence assumes a power to communicate that it does not have. Our timing tires and offends. Whenever we have expectations of others that we do not say directly, we set ourselves up for disappointment. Whenever we try to use silence, or some other form of wordless behavior, to communicate for us, we find ourselves increasingly alienated from those in our environment. Whenever we assume that others know what we are thinking and feeling without our directly telling them, the distance between us will grow and misunderstandings will increase. Whenever our words are spoken without thought of another person's readiness to hear them, we will be experienced as cold and uncaring.

In all of these instances words fail their communicative function because too much responsibility for discovering their meaning has been put on the other person: Someone else must find the hidden need that we have only hinted at. Someone else must clearly understand what we have unclearly expressed. Someone else must search for a message that we have shrouded in vagueness. Someone else must wonder and guess what our true feelings are. Someone else must compensate for our verbal insensitivity. In such cases communication is not mutual, so it cannot lead to mutuality in a relationship; it is not honest, so it does not fit well with discipleship.

Speaking in the Light: Verbal Clarity

Behavioral scientists who have studied the way people employ words in human interaction have identified "verbal clarity" as one of the major skills needed for effective communication.[25] Verbal clarity, sometimes called concreteness, involves the ability to speak in a manner that is straightforward and uncomplicated. It implies a style of speaking that is open, honest, congruent with inner beliefs and real feelings. Verbal clarity enables others to understand what we are saying and to make sense of our whole message, unless their own hearing is fogged with an agenda incompatible with good listening. When we are speaking with verbal clarity, others don't go away saying to themselves: "I wonder what she was trying to say?" or "I wonder what he meant by that?"

The skill of verbal clarity presupposes good self-knowledge. In order to be clear to others, we must first be clear to ourselves. Through a process of reflection, we must clarify our true feelings, our honest expectations, our inner message. Only then will we be able to say what we want others to hear, and not what we hope they will catch if we drop enough hints.

Obstacles to Verbal Clarity

There are a number of problem areas associated with communication that often hinder verbal clarity. One of them, *vague speech*, occurs when we talk without ever coming to the point of our message. We might talk in circles, ramble, repeat ourselves, or jump from topic to topic, but we never make clear what it is that we want to say. Our message is clouded or fuzzy and leaves confusion in the minds of those who hear us. Usually this happens because we haven't sufficiently clarified for ourselves what it is that we feel, think or want to communicate. Consequently, we stumble and wander over our words creating real obstacles to understanding instead of pathways. This style of using words annoys people and often causes them to avoid getting into conversations with us. It is as boring to listen to someone who never says anything as it is to listen to someone who says everything 15 times.

Sometimes, we are vague because we are deliberately trying to deceive someone. We don't want them to know the full truth. Like the pharisees in Matthew's gospel, we are trying to manipulate life, to use others for our own gain, to keep secret our real motives and feelings.

Othertimes, we use vagueness to keep people at a distance, particularly if we are insecure or fearful. If we talk in circles we can make sure that others don't get too close to us. Our vagueness is a protection. It keeps us safe in a private world where we don't have to assume any real responsibility for our thoughts and feelings. We have learned to talk without communicating, and we feel safer that way.

Occasionally people are vague and unclear without realizing it. Many people are extroverts. Extroverts think aloud. In order to arrive at their beliefs and to clarify their ideas and feelings, they have to talk.

134

Sometimes extroverts confuse others when they are doing this. Others assume that they mean what they say, as they say it. However, within a few sentences, the message seems to change. Extroverts can employ the skill of verbal clarity simply by clarifying for others what it is they are doing. If they are thinking aloud, and not intending to state a finished thought, it is important to say this. Extroverts can also avoid confusing others, particularly in more formal or public situations, by forcing themselves to reflect more before speaking.

Another problem which hinders verbal clarity is *hesitant speech.* It often plagues those who are shy or unassertive. If we are fearful of being rejected, uneasy about expressing ourselves, or find it difficult to know what to say, our communication might well lack sufficient clarity. Words that are watered down, tentative, hesitant, too slow or barely audible may cause others to avoid taking us seriously. Though we might have very strong feelings and powerful ideas, others will miss their full impact. Intense feelings that are expressed weakly leave others feeling unsure about their importance to the speaker. No matter how exciting an idea, or how pervasive a feeling, if it is expressed in a monotone, it will probably not sound very exciting.

A third problem which obstructs verbal clarity is the *double message.* Not long ago, I was attending a meeting at which a decision needed to be made about the continuation of a specially appointed justice and peace committee. Each person at the meeting was asked to make a statement for or against the continuation of the committee. At one point in the discussion, the following statement was made:

> I really think this committee has done a marvelous job. The members have started peace-promoting activities that no one else could possibly pull together. I don't know how we'd get along without them. Of course, a lot of other groups in the congregation are doing most of those same things in the area of justice and peace. I don't know if we need a special committee for this.

This was not spoken by an extrovert thinking aloud. It was a statement made by someone who did not want the committee to continue, but who did not want to state her opinion openly. Hers was a classic double message: We can't get along without this committee, but we really don't need them.

Double messages are very common. We usually speak them when

we are in conflict about something, often something that we don't want to admit, especially to others. Usually, one of the messages expresses what we really want or mean, and the other one is a cover spoken because we think it is what people want to hear. In the situation above, what the speaker really wanted to recommend was the discontinuation of the committee, but saying that as clearly as she felt it would have been risky. She was aware that the other people at the meeting wanted the committee to continue, and she didn't want to incur their disapproval. A good way to distinguish the real message from the cover is to listen to ourselves when we are talking with people with whom we feel safe: What do we say behind the door after the meeting is over? If it differs from what we said in public, then we are not operating in the light. We are children of the dark. We are not ushering in the kingdom of God.

Double messages put people in a no-win situation. A pastor tells the parish staff that it will operate as a collegial team, but then he controls all the decisions. A woman tells her friends that she wants to spend more time with them, but she is never available when they call. A husband tells his wife to pick the movie they will go to, but gets upset when she doesn't select the one he wanted. A teacher tells her third-graders they can play in the snow at recess, then scolds them for getting wet. A church says it believes in equality and abhors sexism, then continues to assign roles to women that exclude them from full sacramental and ministerial leadership opportunities.

Double messages can be avoided by being honest about our true wants, needs, thoughts and feelings. Double messages almost always frustrate and confuse their recipients and elicit a great deal of "fuzzy" conflict between people.

A final area of difficulty in verbal clarity involves the use of *symbols without words*. Symbols are not poor substitutes for words. Rather, they point to a deep reality that words cannot fully express. But symbols do need words to make the connection between themselves and that which they symbolize. Since symbols cannot fully reveal themselves without words, words are in the service of symbols.

Communication symbols such as gifts, facial expressions, body movements and gestures need words to make their meaning clear. We can tell our parents that we appreciate them by sending them flowers. We can tell our employer that we are furious by ignoring her for days. We can tell a child that we are sorry by buying her an ice-cream cone. We can tell our spouse of our care by making love. In all of these situations we are using symbols: gifts, presence, time, physical expressions. Symbols such as these are good and important supports to communication, but even among those who have a good relationship, they can never be used without clarifying language.

Our parents might delight in the flowers and in the fact that we thought of them. Our employer will very likely feel a chill. The child will probably feel pacified. Our spouse, loved. But none of them will know exactly what our heart is holding unless we say the words. Gifts, no matter how welcome, can never convey the depth of gratitude that words can name. Ignoring someone, walking around in hostile silence, rarely has the desired effect. Hugs and tears and ice-cream cones can never fully heal wounds or make clear the pain. Sharing silent expressions of love in the night will not sustain a relationship over time.

We need words, clear words, honest words, well-timed words, to give meaning to even our most treasured symbols: "Mom and Dad, the flowers mean that I love you more than I will ever be able to say . . . ." "Joan, I feel so upset that it is hard for me even to talk to you . . . ." "Honey, I'm sorry I yelled at you. I was angry, but you are so special to me and I don't ever want to hurt you . . . ." "I am so in love with you. My love seems to grow stronger and stronger as the years go by. . . ."

Words like these are revealing words. They make known something that is deep inside us—our truth, God's word of truth planted in our hearts. God's word, lighting up windows. Shouting from rooftops. Announcing the arrival of a kingdom that is as marvelous as making love and as ordinary as an apology.

Verbal Clarity: A Skill That Needs Compassion

Verbal clarity is important to accurate and effective communication. It takes the haziness out of our message as we struggle to make that message clear to one another. At the same time, accuracy or effectiveness in communication cannot be the final goal of the Christian. Nuclear warheads are accurate; they are also destructive. Computers are effective, but impersonal. Verbal clarity without listening can be inappropriate. It can lead us to say things that are as out of place as they are clear. Verbal clarity without feeling can be insensitive. Verbal clarity without caring can be blunt and cruel, far removed from the verbal style of the compassionate carpenter from Nazareth.

Without an attachment to all of the other vital skills of human communication verbal clarity can easily turn words into weapons. In order to serve the Christian function of communication, verbal clarity must be as reflective as it is expressive, as gentle as it is honest, and as attentive to others as it is to its own message.

In Service of the Word

As Christians we have a commitment to the word—the word that is Jesus. We have a commitment to the way of life that his words articulate. The early Christians felt that commitment keenly:

> "We will . . . continue to devote ourselves to prayer and to
> the service of the word" (Acts 6:3-4).

For them, service of the word meant preaching, proclaiming Jesus to all who would listen. But before that word could be proclaimed, it had to be lived. It had to become embodied in the life of the preacher. It had to become flesh.

It is only when words become flesh, real and warm embodiments of our inner being, that they can actually communicate something. It is only when they express the deep-down truth of who we are that they have the power to effect goodness: power to heal, power to instruct, power to reconcile, power to express love.

For the evangelist John, it was particularly important that the disciples of Jesus carry on his word. That word had to take root in their hearts and grow. They would remember it, hold fast to it, suffer for it. And through their remembering and their suffering, that word would continue to speak to the world.

John makes it clear that the words of the disciples would have the same function as the words of Jesus—to bring others into the experience of the kingdom of God:

> Remember the words I said to you:
> A servant is not greater than his master.
> If they persecuted me,
> they will persecute you too;
> if they kept my word,
> they will keep yours as well (Jn 15:20).

> Many Samaritans of that town had believed in him on the
> strength of the woman's testimony (Jn 4:39).

138

I pray not only for these,
but for those also
who through their words
will believe in me (Jn 17:20).

Through the strength of the words of the disciples, others would come to faith. Today, we are those disciples. Through the strength of our words, others will come to faith. Through the integrity of our words, others will come to trust. Through the compassion of our words, others will come to healing. And the kingdom of God will come bursting unexpectedly into their lives.

9

WHAT WERE YOU ARGUING ABOUT ON THE ROAD?

Conflict in Relationships

They came to Capernaum, and when he was in the house he asked them, "What were you arguing about on the road?" They said nothing because they had been arguing which of them was the greatest. So he sat down, called the Twelve to him and said, "If anyone wants to be first, he must make himself last of all and servant of all" (Mk 9:33-35).

It is a familiar scene. Even among the followers of Jesus, among the ministers of the kingdom, tensions arise. There are jealousies. One person threatens another. Subtle comparisons are made. Personal insecurities become sources of interpersonal distance even among the most committed of people. It happens at routine times and in common places—in the kitchen, at the office, along the road. Something triggers tension and we move into a stance of self-protection. We become defensive. We say something harsh. We argue. And, like the disciples of Jesus, we don't want to talk about it. It is embarrassing to expose our needs. We don't want anyone to see our vulnerability.

The scene at Capernaum sheds light on one of the primary sources of human conflict: power. Who has it and who doesn't? Who has more of it and who has less of it? The disciple's question, Who is the greatest?, is really a question of power. Who, among all the disciples of Jesus, has the most power? Who walks with Jesus most frequently as they journey the Galilean countryside? Who spends the most time with him? In

141

whom does Jesus confide? To whom do the crowds address their questions? Whose ideas are the most influential in the circle of disciples?
Who catches on most easily to Jesus' teachings? Whose jokes receive the
loudest laughter? Who has the money?

Who is the greatest? We can call it competition or rivalry or insecurity or the quest for achievement. But in the end, their conflict was generated by a desire for power.

Why were the disciples of Jesus preoccupied with thoughts of personal greatness? Why did they care who was first? Why did the followers of the man who had rejected all claims to power in the wilderness want it so badly for themselves?

To answer these questions we need to look at the society in which
Jesus and his disciples lived. Theirs was a world permeated with a system which rank-ordered people, animals and things and assigned
greater value to those at the top and lesser value to those at the bottom.
In the Jewish religious tradition men had more value than women, male
children had more value than female children, children had more value
than slaves. The Israelites had more value than the Samaritans. The
healthy had more value than the deformed. Oxen had more value than
swine.

This practice of viewing everyone and everything through hierarchical glasses strongly influenced the way people thought, including the
disciples of Jesus and also the early Christians for whom the evangelists
wrote. They thought hierarchically: first to last, higher to lower, greatest to least. The people of Jesus' day were neither the first nor the only
people to order creation hierarchically. Others include Plato, Aristotle,
St. Thomas Aquinas, Hitler and the Ku Klux Klan.

In a hierarchical system those at the top not only have greater value, they also have more power. They can influence others, make decisions unilaterally, command greater respect, gather and control more resources. Those were all aspects of "greatness" that not only attracted the
disciples but brought them into direct conflict. Why? Because whenever
someone is greatest someone else has to be least. Whenever someone is
first, someone else has to be last. In a hierarchically valued society, least
and last are not desirable rankings.

And yet that is exactly what Jesus suggests that his disciples should
be: If you want to be first be last. If you want to be greatest of all, be
the lowest (servant). Jesus is not suggesting that the disciples devalue
themselves. He is not encouraging them to have false humility or poor

142

self-concepts. He is not asking them to huddle in the background or hide at the fringes of life. He is saying more about the mentality of hierarchy than he is saying about the individual behavior patterns of his small circle of followers at Capernaum.

Jesus is inviting all of his hearers to get out from under the hierarchical pecking order, to render it meaningless by stepping to the bottom of the scale, to disregard a system which assigns rank-order values to God's all valuable creation.

It is interesting that Jesus does not chide his disciples for arguing in the first place. Actually, the Greek word *dialogizomai* which appears in some translations as "arguing" can also be translated "discussing" or "questioning." The word does not suggest a heated argument as much as it suggests a serious discussion among those who have a vested interest in a topic, a discussion which could lead to differences of opinion.

Mark's presentation of the argument along the road suggests that it is not the fact of arguing, but rather the source of that argument that evokes Jesus' intervention. The source was a power struggle among those who had been hearing about a discipleship of equals where power was shared rather than claimed for oneself.

When Jesus confronted the disciples "they said nothing." They were silent, silent and no doubt embarrassed, because they were grasping for hierarchical power in the face of one whose life was devoted to empowering others; silent because deep down they knew that they were more influenced by the values of the world than the values of God's kingdom.

Power has many faces. It can free or enslave, uplift or oppress, promote peace or generate conflict. Jesus is not opposed to power, but to its abuses. He is opposed to a social and religious system that enslaves the poor, oppresses certain groups, and evokes competition and rivalry for slots on the hierarchical ladder of greatness.

It was conflict related to power-seeking that compelled Jesus to speak. Instead of solving the problem for his disciples, he changed it. The problem was not that they were arguing. The problem was not who was the greatest. The problem was their style of thinking. Theirs was a mentality that would automatically generate conflict because it was a mentality that assumed inequality among people. As long as they were concerned about their own relative importance and rank, they would be in conflict, a kind of conflict that had no relationship to the kingdom of God. Jesus was asking for a radical shift in the way the disciples thought, a shift from thinking in terms of hierarchy to thinking in terms of equality.

What Are You Arguing About?

There are many different types of arguments and different levels of conflict. The friends and disciples of Jesus experienced all of these as they travelled and worked with one another day after day. Like any group of people with differing needs, personalities and mannerisms, they woud have known minor irritations, routine disagreements, and even major divisions. We do not have any record that Jesus attempted to eliminate conflicts or silence arguments among his disciples. In fact, the opposite is true: He didn't want to stop conflict, but to talk about it. Conflict was not ignored, but used as a source of self-knowledge and insight. The evangelists used argument scenes to reveal some important aspect of Jesus' teaching and to make the characteristics of the kingdom vision more clear.

What were you arguing about on the road? What is it that divides you? What is the underlying source of your tension? Is your concern one of the kingdom or one of this world? Can you bring it into the open and talk about it? Can you get a glimpse of the deeply ingrained needs and motives that lie below the surface of the problem? How much of the conflict is caused by your mentality? By the style in which you think?

These were the questions Jesus posed to his disciples. These were the questions the evangelist Mark wanted to ask the first-century readers of his gospel. These are the questions psychologists ask when faced with a 20th-century argument along the road. They are the same questions that you and I must ask ourselves when we are in conflict with the brothers and sisters of our own journey.

Jesus asks a hard thing of his followers: He asks us to examine the sources of our conflicts and to talk about them aloud.

Sources of Human Conflict: Within Me

What are some of the sources of human conflict? What evokes tension in relationships? We can think broadly of two primary sources of conflict: ourselves and our environments.

Conflict can originate within us because of our values, convictions, needs, feelings or physical state. We can precipitate conflict in some of the following instances:

> — I march in a parade protesting the arms race. My relatives
> become upset with me. My value, which says that building

weapons for war is morally wrong, leads to behavior (protesting) which generates conflict with those who have opposing values.

— I monopolize the conversation. My friends dislike it. My excessive need for attention leads to behavior (talking too much) which generates conflict with those who would also like to talk.

— I do not talk to my husband for three days. By the third day he says he's had it. My anger, which is being poorly expressed, leads to behavior (hostile silence) which generates conflict with someone who is the object of my hostility.

— I become dizzy while driving and hit a parked car. The owner of the car is furious. My physical state (dizziness) led to behavior (impaired driving) which generated conflict with a total stranger.

In each of these instances the value, feeling, need, or physical state expressed itself in behavior. Yet the primary source of the conflict was not actually the behavior, but the underlying cause of that behavior. Of course, even in these situations the other persons involved can contribute to the degree of conflict generated. For example, in the first situation, the opposing values of the relatives also add to the source of the conflict. However, it was the original value, expressed in behavior, that actually precipitated the conflict or caused it to surface in the first place.

In each case the conflict can be avoidable or unavoidable, growthful or destructive, handled well or handled poorly. It can be reflected upon and chosen, or not foreseen at all.

What is important is that we think about our behavior and be aware of its underlying motivational forces as well as its effect upon others. In some instances we might decide that standing up for our values, or verbalizing our anger, is worth the conflict that might result. However, if our behavior generates conflict that simply drains people of energy and has no particular potential for growth, then we need to take a serious look at changing our behavior and reducing or eliminating the conflict source.

In the earlier example the need for power led to the behavior of arguing among the disciples. Jesus suggested to them that they re-examine their needs and reorder their values because the kind of conflict that their needs generated was not helpful to the witness of the kingdom vision. Likewise there are times when we must re-examine needs and reorder values, particularly if they generate the kind of conflict that does not serve the gospel.

Jesus generated conflict. So did Judas. So did Mary of Bethany. So did Paul. In each instance the source was different. Jesus provoked conflict because his values and vision came into direct opposition with those of the religious establishment. Judas generated conflict apparently because of greed. Mary of Bethany generated conflict because she did not conform to socially accepted standards of behavior in public. Paul generated conflict because his own strong convictions and fiery personality were not always well integrated. Some conflicts serve the gospel. Some do not.

Sources of Human Conflict: Within the Environment

Sometimes the primary precipitating cause of conflict is in the environment, in persons or things outside ourselves. Such conflicts can be caused by healthy personal differences, by the unhealthy behavior patterns of others, or by a variety of other situations beyond our control:

— I prefer to go to the mountains for vacation, and my wife prefers to visit relatives. Conflict is generated among those with healthy personal differences.

— A friend becomes drunk and insults other guests at my home. My friend's unhealthy behavior (getting drunk and being abusive) generates conflict among those who have done nothing to provoke it. The source of the problem is within my friend.

— The pastor of our parish has serious personality problems and finds security in clinging to the past and fighting renewal. Parish members find themselves in a constant situation of conflict with him over most aspects of parish life.

Most interpersonal conflicts are not so clear and clean-cut that they can be reduced to single underlying causes. Usually there are a number of interacting factors, needs, feelings and circumstances that affect the intensity and duration of conflict situations.

What is important is that we reflect on our own life and relationships, and on our responses to the conflicts in which we find ourselves. We need to ask ourselves the questions that Jesus asked the disciples along the road:

What am I arguing about? Why am I involved in this particular conflict? What needs, values and feelings do I have that are contributing to, or precipitating the conflict? Are those needs, values and feelings healthy or unhealthy? of normal intensity or excessively strong? Is the conflict draining and destructive to myself and others or is there some value to it? some potential for growth? some cause worth the risk and worthy of the gospel?

The following outline might be helpful in reflecting on these questions:

CONFLICT SOURCES

Healthy & Normal Differences:	Behaviors:	Feelings:	Situations:
Personality	Manipulative	Anger	Fatigue
Values	Controlling	Jealousy	Illness
Perceptions	Obnoxious	Threat	Hunger
Taste	Abusive	Oppression	Danger
Preferences	Violent	Confusion	Loss
Age	Dishonest	Powerlessness	Mental Illness
Needs	Selfish	Loneliness	War
Other healthy	Destructive	Guilt	Personal Need
differences	Cruel	Insecurity	Accident

CONFLICT CYCLE

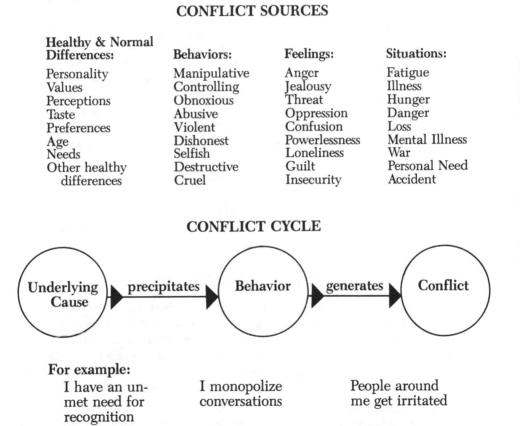

For example:
I have an un-   I monopolize   People around
met need for   conversations   me get irritated
recognition

Whatever its source, one of the reasons that talking about conflict is often so painful and difficult is that most of the *feelings* that surround conflict situations are so uncomfortable—fear, embarrassment, anger,

147

hurt, confusion, insecurity, helplessness, guilt. We fear losing face, losing control, being rejected. We will be embarrassed if we cry. We want to protect ourselves from further pain. We don't know what to say or how to start talking about the conflict. We are not sure if talking will do any good. We shouldn't be upset about this in the first place. It would probably be easier to ignore the whole thing and cope with the conflict rather than try to reconcile or resolve it.

Conflict As the Norm in Relationships

We often expend more energy fighting the *fact* that we are in conflict than we do taking steps to resolve it. We shun the reality of conflict as though it were something that should not be happening. Actually, conflict in relationships is the *norm* rather than the exception. If conflict can be generated by those with healthy personal differences, then whenever two or more people occupy the same general space for even a brief duration of time the possibility of conflict arises. The longer the span of time spent interacting, the greater is the possibility of conflict. Unless we live in extreme isolation, either physically or emotionally, sooner or later we will experience conflict. We will find ourselves arguing along the road.

Conflict, then, is both normal and inevitable in relationships. It is part of the human condition. Every conflict situation holds some potential, some possibility for growth in self-knowledge, and possibly for growth in intimacy. It also holds potential for destruction. The choice is ours.

Conflict and Personal Growth

Conflict is more apt to result in growth if it is talked about among those involved, a fact that Jesus seemed to know. Yet talking about our conflicts directly with those involved in them is often the last thing we do. It is far easier to talk to the relatives, the neighbors, even the bartender than it is to talk to the person with whom we are in tension. This avoidance usually prolongs the conflict and heightens the tension.

If we examine the sources of our conflict we can deepen our own self-awareness and come to make important changes in our manner and lifestyle. Carol was a person who did just that. She was 45 when she acknowledged to herself for the first time that her life reflected more conflicts than other people seemed to have—a hard fact to admit. In spite of a reasonably happy marriage and homelife, Carol was always at odds with someone. Several times each year there were blowups: with Aunt Millie, with her daughter's third-grade teacher, with the associate pastor, with Mrs. Jones next door, with various in-laws, neighbors and friends. Finally, during a particularly unpleasant tiff with a co-worker on a church committee, the co-worker told Carol that she could no longer work with her, that she could not handle the tension that seemed to characterize so many of Carol's relationships. Carol could have dismissed the co-worker's comments as "her problem," but in a rare moment of self-reflection she thought about what had been said. She looked back over her life and had to admit that fights, tensions and negative interactions did seem characteristic for her. Over a period of time Carol began to realize that it was she who precipitated these conflicts, and that most of them served no real purpose. Rather, they reflected her deep-seated feeling of inadequacy—and a resultant tendency to cling to her own ideas and attempt to control other people.

In this instance Carol's lifelong pattern of conflict with others served as a source of revelation for her, a guidepost that alerted her to the fact that something was wrong. Somethings was missing in her own life, and it was generating conflicts that hurt her relationships. Once Carol identified the unmet need for self-esteem in her own life, she could meet that need more appropriately. She gave up trying to gain a feeling of importance and usefulness by controlling other people's lives.

When conflicts are faced, growth can occur. When they are not faced, growth does not occur. Often it is feedback from others that can serve as sources of revelation, moments of grace. But we have to *hear* what others are saying, think about it, search for truth, however painful. Too often painful feedback is dismissed without reflection. It is regarded as untrue without so much as a thought. It is usually easier and more comfortable to assume that any painful feedback is coming out of the other person's anger or poor judgment, rather than out of the truth of our own life.

Facing Conflict

Facing conflict means just what it says—it means to literally *look it in the face*. It means to own it. To explore it. To make decisions about it. Owning conflict means admitting that it exists in the first place. We do not deny it or pretend that it will go away if we ignore it long enough. Owning conflict also means that we assume at least some of the responsibility for it. We do not assume that it is *all* the other person's fault. We may say: "I am in conflict with Bob Smith. There are probably some things that I am doing which helped to generate this conflict or keep it from getting resolved." Next, we begin to explore the situation—to think about it. This requires that we ask some hard questions:

— What is the external cause of the conflict? Or, what is the behavior that is visible?

— How am I behaving? How is the other person behaving?

— Is any dimension of my behavior making the conflict worse? keeping it from being resolved? What am I doing that is hard for the other person to handle?

— What is the *underlying cause* of the conflict? the needs that I have that lie below the surface? (Don't be fooled with this one—if I am in conflict, I have needs that are being threatened.) What might some of the other person's needs be?

— How serious is the conflict? life and death proportions? very serious? moderately serious? minor?

— Is my behavior appropriate (proportionate) to the severity of the conflict? (If I am not speaking to someone who borrowed my pen without asking, my behavioral response is disproportionate to the offense; I am overreacting. If, on the other hand, I continue to cook and clean for someone who beats me, my behavioral response is disproportionate in the other extreme; I am underreacting.)

— How long has the conflict gone on?

— What have I done (or we done) to try and resolve it?

— What purpose is the conflict serving? (Again, don't be fooled. Sometimes I can get a lot of secondary gain by being in a perpetual conflict situation. I can get attention, sympathy, avoid responsibility, fulfill a need to be punished or be victimized, avoid intimacy.)

— Who else is affected by the conflict? What is the conflict doing to others in the environment? Is it fair to them?

— What responsibility do I have in response to this conflict?

Finally, once the issue has been thoroughly explored, some kind of decision is called for. This is the part of facing conflict that is most apt to be omitted. It is common to simply tolerate the conflict and never really make a clear decision to do something about it. The decision-making process involves some of the following questions and steps:

— Is the conflict resolvable or reconcilable? Is it realistic to work toward a resolution?

— What would have to happen for the conflict to end? What would I have to do? What would the other person(s) have to do?

— What level of commitment exists to resolve the conflict? on my part? on the other person's part?

— What am I (are we) willing to do to become reconciled?

— What am I (are we) not willing to do?

— If I judge the conflict to be reconcilable, exactly what will I make a commitment to do? by what date?

There are some conflicts, unfortunately, that simply are not resolvable. There are others that might eventually be resolved, but not without some form of outside help. It is important that individuals distinguish between conflicts that are:

— Resolvable by talking thing out among those directly involved in the conflict.

— Possibly resolvable with an outside facilitator.

— Not resolvable.

Otherwise, a great deal of energy can be wasted trying to fix something that cannot be fixed. That only leads to frustration and often to an intensification of the conflict.

Conflicts that stand the optimum chance for resolution are those which involve personal differences among essentially healthy people. Such people are usually capable of expressing their honest feelings, listening without interrupting, and seeing reality without distortion—all essential characteristics for effective conflict resolution. With enough talking, patience and mutual respect even serious conflicts based on differing values, perceptions, need preferences and personality traits can often be reconciled.

Confronting conflict situations means sharing our feelings about the tensions we are experiencing directly and in a supportive manner. Put simply, confrontation or conflict resolution means that we talk about the tension points in our lives. Talking can clarify the problem, relieve tension, and prevent uncomfortable feelings from building up.

The Purpose of Confrontation

The purpose of confrontation is not to change the other person, but to open up the issue, to bring tensions and problems into the light. Confrontation is not an attempt to get the other person to see things our way, but to give verbal expression to our honest feelings and enable the other person(s) to do the same. This presupposes that we talk about the feelings as clearly as possible: "Last night I felt really hurt when you laughed at what I was trying to say. . . ." "It seems that we are avoiding each other lately . . . ." "Right now, I'm starting to feel defensive and I don't like that feeling . . . ." "I know we need to talk but I'm so afraid of saying the wrong thing. I don't know where to start . . . ." "Whenever we are together, it seems that we start picking at each other. I sense that something I do is irritating you . . . ." "I get so upset when I am talking and you interrupt me in the middle of a sentence."

In genuine conflict management, it is important that we take responsibility for our own feelings: admit them, and name them aloud without rambling on and on or giving justifications for them. It is also important that we do not attribute our negative feelings to the other person. They are ours. The other has not caused them. We might experience the feelings in response to something another person does, but they are still our feelings and our responsibility.

Talking about uncomfortable feelings this openly is difficult and often painful. But if feelings can be discussed without too much defensiveness, the result is often not only a lessening of the conflict, but a growth in intimacy. It is well-managed conflict and openly confronted feelings that lead to increased closeness. As honest feelings are faced and conflicts are explored, we become more vulnerable to each other—the very process which leads to progressive intimacy. People who cannot deal effectively with conflict in their lives rarely experience intimacy.

When Conflicts Cannot Be Resolved

Some conflicts cannot be resolved or reconciled without the outside support of a facilitator or counselor. Typically, such conflicts are those in which one or more of the persons involved lack the psychological health needed to engage in productive conversation. This is true if one or more of the persons:

— deny any responsibility for the conflict or blame others.

— cannot admit or express feelings.

— cannot listen without interrupting.

— tend to distort reality or to misinterpret what others say.

— have noticeable psychological symptoms (severe depression, severe anxiety, paranoid ideas, loss of touch with reality, uncontrollable outbursts of temper or a tendency to physical attack).

— are currently abusing drugs or alcohol.

Whenever psychological illness is present among those in conflict, the lack of wellness will certainly inhibit any attempt at reconciliation. Many people know the futility of struggling alone with a husband who cannot express his feelings, a pastor who dominates all conversations, a wife who lashes out accusations and judgments, a relative who is suspicious of another's intentions, or a companion who leaves the room every time conflict situations are verbalized. Too often, attempts are made to talk about conflicts with people who are not emotionally equipped to handle that kind of interpersonal exchange. Their everyday behavior is already saying that they cannot handle themselves, much less respond to anyone else's pain.

In such situations it can be helpful to bring in a third party to facilitate discussions about conflict—if all involved are willing. In those cases where one of the persons refuses to seek outside help, those who do wish to resolve the conflict can still seek guidance from a professional counselor. A good therapist can often suggest ways of dealing with difficult or emotionally ill people. Sometimes a conflict with an ill person can be made worse by the way we respond to him or her. Talking with an outside professional can help us respond in such a way that chances for reconciliation are maximized. It can also provide some much needed support.

What about those situations involving irreconcilable conflict? What do we do when we are in a situation where there is no possible hope of resolving differences or minimizing tensions? How do we determine that a conflict is not resolvable?

There are situations where it does not seem possible to resolve or even reduce conflict between individuals. Expending energy at conflict resolution is not helpful in such situations. These include:

— Situations where the person(s) who is the primary source of the conflict does not want reconciliation and rejects all attempts at conflict resolution.

— Situations where the person(s) who is the primary source of the conflict is incapable of eliminating or changing the behavior that precipitates the conflict.

— Environments or situations containing sources of conflict that are beyond our capacity to influence or change.

What does one do in these seemingly hopeless situations? Aside from praying for the direct intervention of God, there are really only three broad options: We can leave the environment; we can decide on a coping strategy; or we can attack and fight.

Choosing the Best Option in a No-Win Situation

The first option, *environmental transfer,* is rarely an easy decision to make. Initially it often appears impossible, though often it offers the greatest possibility of health for all concerned. It means that a person leaves that which is familiar and secure: a job, a home, a geographic location, a husband or wife. It means uprooting, starting over, changing—all at a time when the individual is sapped of energy.

There are many situations where individuals feel trapped in long-term conflict that does not appear to offer any way out: destructive marriages, intolerable living situations, unbearable jobs, hostile relationships. Living and working in such circumstances saps both personal energy and self-respect. It often severely impairs a person's capacity for seeing other options. It becomes easier to view the situation as unchangeable than to take the initiative to get out of it.

Whenever a relationship, a job or living situation becomes dehumanizing to such an extent that the individual feels in a constant state of tension—has increasing apathy, depression and helplessness, or is physically, verbally or emotionally abused—then these conditions are clues, signs, bits of revelation calling for change. Sometimes that change requires terminating a relationship, leaving a marriage, quitting a job, or moving to a different living situation. It is not holy to tolerate abuse when there is a way out. It is not virtuous to stick with a situation until all energy has been drained and all self-esteem lost.

Unless we happen to be prisoners in a concentration camp, or some other equally confining situation, we have responsibility to maximize our chances for personal growth. That does not mean that we neglect others or become self-indulgent. Nor does it mean that we move or leave everytime there is pain or conflict. It means that we assess the situation, that we do everything reasonably possible to bring growth out of conflict, that we try to work toward reconciliation. But when we realize that a conflict is not reconcilable, we do not settle into the role of passive victim.

When environmental transfer is clearly not a good or a possible solution to an irreconcilable conflict, it becomes necessary to adjust our expectations. Instead of working toward resolution, we attempt to manage the conflict in the best way that we can. This process has some clear steps:

— We make a conscious decision to live with the problem.

— We stop complaining about the problem. (This demands a cessation of all gossip, all negative comments, all judgmental thinking.)

— We make a decision not to feel sorry for ourselves or to become a martyr.

— We eliminate all conscious plans and efforts to resolve the conflict. We accept the fact that things won't change.

— We list coping strategies, ways that will help us survive better and minimize our emotional drain.

Coping strategies include all those things that support us in our effort to stay in a difficult situation without being debilitated by it. They help us keep perspective, broaden our base of support and maintain a sense of self-respect. Coping strategies include talking about our situation with a trusted friend or counselor on a regular basis, starting a new hobby, engaging in regular physical activity or bioenergetic exercise, becoming involved in an outside project, taking regular time away from the difficult situation, or doing anything that feels energizing and helpful.

When people are immersed in a difficult situation, very often all of their energy is consumed coping with the problem. If there is no outside source of energy, they become chronically fatigued and depressed. This makes reaching outside of the painful environment even more difficult. Too often it seems like too much trouble. Yet, it is precisely at such times that people most need to turn outward.

Managing Anger When Conflict Is Chronic

When a person is in a chronically difficult situation, anger is usually evoked on a regular basis. Because talking about it with the person involved is not an option in this case, it often seems that there is no way to release the anger. This is when physical exercise can be particularly helpful. Studies have shown that regular physical activity can reduce the tension and tight body state that accompany persistent anger. Aerobic exercise, jogging, swimming, fast walking, bicycling and other active sports are especially good. Including vocal sound such as yelling, cheering, deep breathing and groaning gives added and beneficial release. Activities such as reading, listening to music or watching television are not helpful because they are too passive. They are distractions from anger rather than expressions of anger energy. Anger mobilizes the whole body and unless the whole body is involved in the exercise it is not as helpful. Of course, engaging in regular physical exercise should be part of everyone's total wellness program. It should not be reserved just for anger.

Bioenergetic exercises such as pillow pounding or working with a punching bag are also very helpful, especially for those who tend to deal with their anger in very passive ways. Some people have ridiculed bioenergetics and claimed that these exercises are childish and unnecessary. However studies have shown that bioenergetics is extremely useful in enabling people to acknowledge strong anger. The person who pounds a pillow is less apt to pound another person.

In some conflict situations the people involved do not consider leaving the environment, nor do they consider coping strategies. They simply maintain a perpetual state of open hostility. They declare war. Such an interpersonal war has winning as its aim. It does not seek to reconcile or resolve conflicts but to get back at the person who is the object of the anger. It is characterized by ongoing arguments, shouting matches, verbal abuse, criticism, sarcasm, manipulation, hidden agendas and maximum defensiveness. As in any war, the combatants try to obtain allies and often succeed in turning relatives, friends and even children against each other. They do almost anything to prove their own point of view, to show the error of the other, to come out the victor. They even experience a sense of delight when the other is hurt, humiliated or put down.

Another more subtle type of interpersonal warfare is the cold war. The individuals are in sharp conflict, but they deal with it only indirectly. In such situations there is a polite, though hostile distance characterized by cool silence, brief or curt comments, sharp vocal tone, physical withdrawal, ignoring, blank or angry glances, and veiled attempts to make the other feel unimportant.

When interpersonal fighting, whether open or covert, is used to deal with conflict, the problems only escalate. Yet this method is very common in families, offices, convents, rectories and schools. Rather than bringing conflict into the open and taking positive steps toward reconciliation, many people seem to get locked into perpetual warfare with each other. As a result they are drained of energy, they are distracted from other interests, and they create a tense, negative environment for others.

Not all fighting is destructive. At times it is appropriate to stand up for our rights, to disagree, and to fight for what we believe. Such fighting ought to be fair. We should be respectful of others involved and willing to listen to their point of view. We should avoid deliberately hurting others or taking advantage of their vulnerabilities. We should work toward some kind of resolution and not prolong the fighting indefinitely; there is a difference between fighting *for* something and simply fighting.

Jesus fought for the rights of the oppressed. He fought the laws and religious observances that enslaved people. He fought those who attempted to curtail the freedom of others. He fought for his vision of the kingdom. He did not abuse people. He did not get stalemated in endless struggles to have the last word. He did not engage in dragged-out battles of wit with his enemies. He said what he had to say and did what he had to do. Then he left the situation.

Learning to Manage Conflict More Effectively

Knowing what to do in a conflict situation is never easy. Often it is necessary to try several options before something seems to move the situation toward reconciliation. An important place to start in attempting to improve our manner of dealing with conflict is to have accurate information about anger and all of the other emotions related to conflict. Attending workshops, reading and talking with others can all help to familiarize us with our own emotional responses, assess their degree of health, and better understand why we react the way we do in situations of conflict.

While increasing intellectual information about conflict is important, it will not of itself lead to behavior change. There are many people who go from one workshop to the next, who take part in one personal growth experience after another, who have read every book and listened to every tape on the topic—and show little change in the way they respond to conflict or deal with their emotions from year to year.

An important second step involves moving the information from a head level to a heart level—or a stomach level. It involves going from knowing to doing. It means translating what we know to what we do. For example, if I know in my head that it is important for me to give verbal expression to strong feelings of anger, I need to move from knowing that to doing it. Knowing is easy. Doing is hard.

Doing what we know, moving from head to heart, from information to behavior, is perhaps the most difficult dimension of personal growth and change. It requires, first of all, a decision. We must reflect on what it is that we want to do, and then, at some point and after clear reflection, we must say: "I *will* do this. I *am* going to say my feelings of anger when I experience them, given appropriateness of time, place and manner of expression." As part of such a decision it is helpful to be as specific as possible and to start small. It would be too ambitious to decide to start practicing a new behavior with a person who terrifies us.

Making the clear and conscious choice to do something implies risks—to do some things that might be uncomfortable or unfamiliar. If we wait for the butterflies in our stomach to go away before we talk to someone with whom we are experiencing tension, or if we avoid a confrontation because we are afraid we may not handle it well, we will never learn to be more expressive in regard to conflict. Change comes in the midst of discomfort, and growth often occurs in pain.

Making that initial decision is critical. Making the choice to talk instead of remaining silent the next time we feel angry is part of the link between knowing something and doing it. There are a few general guidelines that can facilitate the process of confrontation once the decision has been made:

— Think before speaking. Practice what you are going to say aloud before you get into the situation.

158

— Keep to the point and be brief. Avoid rambling and repeating.

— Be specific. If someone's behavior is offensive, give clear examples so the person knows what you are talking about.

— Speak slowly. Talking fast adds tension. Make a conscious attempt to slow down.

— Speak in a low tone. Anxiety causes the throat muscles to tighten making the voice pitch higher. A high, shrill tone is offensive.

— Breathe. You may find that you hold your breath or breathe in a very shallow manner when you are anxious. This only increases discomfort. Concentrate on breathing slowly and deeply. You will feel more in control of yourself.

— Look at the person you are addressing. Establish eye contact.

— If you start to feel defensive, say so. ("I feel defensive when you tell me that I don't understand you . . . .")

— Give the other person a chance to talk. Listen without interrupting.

— Listen intently. When the other person is talking, don't think about what you are going to say as soon as he or she stops.

— Talk about your honest feelings and perceptions regarding the situation. Don't accuse, attack or judge.

— Avoid giving the other person advice about what he or she should do.

— If the confrontation gets out of hand, and tempers flare, stop. Don't allow the session to turn into a shouting match. Ask the other person if you can try talking again at a later date. Set the date.

— If the confrontation results in an adequate expression of feelings, ask the other person how he or she feels about the session before you depart.

— Try to make some joint decisions about future actions if that is appropriate. ("Where are we going to go from here?")

— Before terminating the session, thank the other person for listening to you and for expressing his or her views.

We often avoid talking directly about conflict with those involved because we fear the situation will be made worse. Often it is made worse because we lack basic communication skills that enable us to listen to one another with mutual respect. Very few situations will be made worse if we make a sincere attempt to listen to each other's point of view and stick to expressing our feelings without attacking the other.

Entering conflict situations directly instead of avoiding them or passively tolerating them is not only psychologically healthy, it is also Christian. A person who has embraced Christianity automatically embraces the behavior of discipleship. Giving intellectual assent to the kingdom vision is only a small part of the process of living as a Christian. People will not know that we are disciples of Jesus by the accuracy of our dogmas. They will know it by the reconciling love that is visible in our treatment of one another. Part of that loving involves the way we respond to one another when we are in conflict.

Far More Important Than Any Sacrifice

As with other dimensions of behavior, the Christian scriptures do not give us specific rules for dealing with conflict. Rather, they attempt to acquaint us with the broad guidelines of living in the world of relationships as followers of Jesus. The essence of biblical behavioral guidelines is the law of love:

> "Which is the first of all the commandments?" Jesus replied, "This is the first: . . . *you must love the Lord your God with all your heart, with all your soul*, with all your mind and *with all your strength.* The second is this: *You must love your neighbor as yourself.* There is no commandment greater than these." The scribe said to him, . . . "To love him [God] with all your heart, with all your understanding and strength, and to love your neighbor as yourself, this is far more important than any holocaust or sacrifice." Jesus, seeing how wisely he had spoken, said, "You are not far from the kingdom of God" (Mk 12:28-34).

Love one another as you love yourself. It sounds gentle and beautiful. In real life it is demanding and difficult, especially when one moves beyond the softer side of romantic love and encounters conflict.

It is interesting that the commandment of love is presented by all of the synoptic writers within the context of conflict. Jesus has arrived in Jerusalem. The chief priests, the scribes and the elders have questioned his authority. When he continues to teach, they become angry and want to arrest him. Soon some Pharisees and Sadducees gather with trick questions designed to trap him. It is against this backdrop, surrounded by enemies, being tricked, tested and attacked, that Matthew, Mark and Luke present Jesus talking about love. Even in the midst of conflict Jesus does not lose sight of the essence of the kingdom, the greatest of the commandments.

Conflict does not excuse us from loving. Anger toward another does not exempt us from the greatest of the commandments. It calls us to enter conflict with the attitude and behavior of those who have known Jesus, who believe that loving our neighbor is "far more important than any holocaust or sacrifice" (Mk 12:33). Even when that neighbor has attacked us, tricked us or been hostile to us, Christianity demands that we let the law of love guide our response. Such a response does not mean a denial of anger, an avoidance of conflict, or a passive acceptance of a bad situation. It does mean that we face an angry neighbor with behavior that fits with Christian loving: honesty, respect and, above all, a willingness to seek forgiveness.

Leave Your Gift at the Altar

Matthew is particularly strong in his conviction that Jesus demands that we seek reconciliation in response to our anger:

> "So then, if you are bringing your offering to the altar and there remember that your brother has something against you, . . . go and be reconciled with your brother first" (Mt 5:23-24).

Leave your gift at the altar. Go and be reconciled. First. This would have been a very troublesome saying for Matthew's Jewish audience. Cultic responsibility, symbolized by taking a gift to the altar, was of paramount importance. It was the Jew's first duty and could not be subordinated to any other activity. Yet Matthew's Jesus has the audacity to suggest that reconciliation takes precedence over cultic activity! It was more than a new emphasis. It was a whole new attitude. It was a reflection of the attitude echoed earlier by the scribe of Mark's gospel who suggested that love of God, self and neighbor was even more important than holocausts or sacrifice. The centrality of love, expressed in behav-

161

ior, could not be clearer for the disciple of Jesus.

That forgiveness was associated with love is evident in several gospel stories. In fact, love forgives and forgiveness, in turn, enables greater love:

> "There was once a creditor who had two men in his debt; one owed him five hundred denarii, the other, fifty. They were unable to pay, so he pardoned them both. Which of them will love him more?" "The one who was pardoned more, I suppose," answered Simon. Jesus said, "You are right" (Lk 7:41-43).

> "For this reason I tell you that her sins, her many sins, must have been forgiven her, or she would not have shown such great love. It is the man who is forgiven little who shows little love" (Lk 7:47-48).

The experience of forgiveness frees people or loosens them from the bonds that inhibit loving. Forgiveness is an experience of feeling loved by another, loved so much that faults and failures are set aside in favor of the relationship.

How seriously should we associate the readiness to forgive with the great commandment of love? That was Peter's question. It had been hard for him to let go of some of his Jewish traditions, traditions which put a definite limit on the number of times one was expected to forgive an offending brother or sister.

> Then Peter went up to him and said, "Lord, how often must I forgive my brother if he wrongs me? As often as seven times?" Jesus answered, "Not seven, I tell you, but seventy-seven times" (Mt 18:21-22).

No definite number makes forgiveness perfect. I cannot limit my willingness to extend forgiving love toward those who have offended me.

There are times when forgiving someone is easier than at other times. It is not tremendously costly to forgive a friend who has hurt my feelings and sincerely apologizes. My capacity to forgive is not stretched when an offense is minor or does not affect my personal life. But there are situations where forgiveness is the last thing I feel toward someone. Perhaps a person has inflicted deep pain on me or on someone I love.

I once met a young man at a retreat who expanded my concept of biblical forgiveness. He sat in the back of the room during the conferences. At the end of the retreat he came up to talk.

"It has been very hard for me to be here," he confided. "It is always hard for me to hear someone talk about forgiveness in connection with being a good Christian because there is someone in my life that I just cannot forgive."

His story was a painful one. He was born a twin. When he was 16, his twin sister committed suicide. He never understood why. The family never discussed it. A little over a year before, in response to his persistent questioning, his mother finally told him that his sister had been the victim of his older brother's sexual abuse. When she realized she was pregnant, her guilt, fear and confusion resulted in her death. She left a suicide note explaining all—a note that only her parents saw.

For the young man at the retreat, this news had been like a nightmare. He had been unable to speak to his offending brother since he learned the truth of his sister's death. He refused to attend his brother's wedding, stayed away from the family's Christmas celebration, and could feel only cold hatred toward his brother. He also felt a great deal of guilt, a guilt that only intensified when he came face to face with the love demands of the gospel. In the course of our conversation he told me that he was in therapy. He admitted that more than anything he wanted to be able to forgive his brother and to let go of the hatred he felt. He was taking positive steps to reach his goal. Now all he could do was pray, hope and wait for time to bring healing.

This young man taught me that forgiveness, like so many other aspects of life, is often a process. Sometimes, we can forgive in one great act of letting go; other times, we cannot. The pain is too great. Healing takes longer than a moment. But starting the process is the most important part of developing an attitude of forgiveness. Essential to that beginning process is wanting, more than anything, to be able one day to forgive.

Go and Be Reconciled

That young man's intense struggle to expand his capacity to forgive spoke to me about gospel love, a fiery love that pulls us to our limits and beyond, a love that does not expect instant perfection but is patient with us. It is a love that gives us time and offers us compassion and forgiveness even as we wait to forgive, a love that can make us cry out in agony as often as it comforts us. It can leave us alone in the dark as often as it fills us with excitement. Whether we are experiencing the warmth of a fulfilling relationship or are embroiled in the midst of conflict, the love demands of the gospel are there urging us beyond easy romance and limited giving.

Jesus knew the demands of love well. And, as all genuine lovers do, he knew the reality of conflict. He knew the bitter taste of a friend's betrayal. He seethed with rage in response to the Temple abusers. He was irritated with Martha's kitchen frenzy. He had repeated encounters with hostile members of the religious establishment. Jesus got miffed, irritated, frustrated, upset and filled with rage.

The gospel writers could have easily eliminated the examples of an angry Messiah. Writing at least 20 years after his death they could have deemphasized the conflicts of his life. But they chose to present him facing conflict rather than shunning it. They chose to stand him in the midst of broken relationships and violent people. He had conflict with Peter, conflict with Judas, conflict with his relatives, conflict with religious leaders, conflict with traditions, conflict with the crowds. And in the midst of it all we are told that he did not seek revenge or retaliation. He faced conflict. He named the tension areas of his life. He owned his anger and expressed it in a variety of ways.

And standing there in the midst of opposition, struggling with his friends and clashing with his enemies, he talks of love. We hear of a forgiving father who rushes out to meet the son who has disappointed him, of a weary shepherd who goes out in search of a single stray, of a woman caught in adultery who experiences acceptance instead of stoning, of a criminal who dies knowing the compassion of forgiveness. Stories of people in conflict. Parents and children. Workers. Lovers. Sinners. They are our stories. They are told to remind us that we cannot have life without conflict, and that conflict holds out opportunities to us: opportunities to recover something that has been lost, opportunities to heal, opportunities to turn our lives around, opportunities to come home.

10

HE EMPTIED HIMSELF

Self-Acceptance and Self-Disclosure

His state was divine,
yet he did not cling
to his equality with God
but emptied himself
to assume the condition of a slave (Phil 2:6).

Kenosis. To empty out. A familiar Greek word and an often heard expression in spirituality. Among Christians, *kenosis* has come to mean the process of self-emptying demanded of the followers of Jesus. For many, however, it has defined a kind of literal self-negation thought necessary for true holiness: putting the desires of others first, disregarding personal needs, offering up, giving in, and bearing pain in silence. Life certainly does offer opportunities for holy self-denial. But when self-emptying becomes self-negation, it is not an embrace of fuller Christianity but a distortion of it.

Some spiritualities of the past have understood the kenosis of Jesus in just such a distorted way. He was often portrayed as empty of any qualities that would identify him as a human being: empty of spontaneous feelings, empty of a distinctive personality with unique personal tastes, preferences and traits. It was easy to think of such a Jesus as distinctly set apart from the real human race, as some kind of spiritual robot whose divine computer enabled him to consistently deny any serious involvement with his flesh.

History, even to our present day, shows that more than a few spiritual writers and church officials have been uncomfortable with the humanity of Jesus. At the same time, they could not deny it without lapsing into heresy. One way of dealing with this dilemma has been to acknowledge the humanity of Jesus in passing and then focus serious theological reflection on his divinity. Defending Jesus' humanity while avoiding any attempt to spell it out too specifically or too humanly has been an effective way to keep Jesus of Nazareth "in the flesh" but not really of it. Presenting him as a divine human who "emptied himself" has, in much of the practical spirituality of the past, given us a savior emptied of his humanity, and certainly emptied of any suggestion of the sexual dimension of that humanity.

There are still many people who are ambivalent about the expressed humanity of Jesus. "Yes, Jesus Christ was a full human person," they will say. But take a closer look at what being a full human person means, and many of these same individuals begin to squirm. Suggest that the human Jesus struggled like any other person to know what direction his life should take, and some will reply that his infused knowledge eliminated such a struggle. Suggest that the human Jesus genuinely needed the companionship of friends, and some will say that Jesus involved himself in friendships on earth not because he really needed them, but because he wished to set an example for us. Suggest that the human Jesus actually felt hungry, discouraged, angry, lonely or impatient and there will be some who quickly defend his apparent digression into these human feelings as utterly selfless and, therefore, not fully human. Suggest that the human Jesus felt sexual desire as would any normal human person, and someone will anxiously cite his virginity, but a virginity characterized more by asexuality than by a carefully searched choice made by a sexually responsive adult who had grown through all of the normal stages of psychosexual development. Suggest a picture of Jesus that is too human for comfort, and Paul's phrase, "He emptied himself" becomes, for some, a theologically acceptable way out. Jesus had a human nature, but he "emptied himself" of its full expression.

We deny to Jesus what we are most uneasy with in ourselves. In throwing a cloak of divinity over the human characteristics of Jesus we provide excuses for distancing ourselves from our own humanness. When we divert our attention from the expressed humanity of Jesus, we can easily divert ourselves from our own humanity.

Growing in Christian love is then too easily equated with movement away from the human and, more specifically, away from the self. The feelings, needs and desires of the "human" self thus become enemies to the "spiritual" self. In an attempt to remove anything considered an obstacle to true Christian holiness, sincere Christians have often become

166

seriously alienated from their deepest selves, unaware of the needs that lie deep beneath the surface motivating much of their behavior. In the interest of the kind of biblical self-emptying that they believe to be characteristic of the kenosis of Jesus, they develop a pattern of behavior that is dangerously lacking in self-awareness and self-reflection. It is this pattern of poor self-awareness that leads to the hurtful behaviors we experience as selfishness in others, and which others experience as selfishness in us.

When genuine biblical kenosis degenerates into denial for denial's sake, or provides an outlet for the expression of low self-worth, then it is not a virtue. It is a symptom of personal pathology. When self-emptying flows out of guilt, a desire to please others, or an unhealthy understanding of Christian sacrifice, it easily becomes a pathway to rigidity, self-righteousness, and a state of psychological emptiness that bears little resemblance to gospel spirituality.

"He emptied himself to assume the condition of a slave." Paul was writing in the context of an early hymn in praise of Christ's total acceptance of his humanity, of his fidelity to his human condition. Jesus emptied himself of anything that would have blunted the full experience of being human in the world. To interpret the kenosis of Jesus as the complete denial of his own needs or as the rejection of any dimension of what it meant for him to be truly and fully human is to distort the deepest meaning of his sacrifice.

The true kenosis of Jesus lay not in self-negation but in self-embrace, saying a consistent and honest yes to all the demands that being fully human made on him. "He did not cling to his equality with God," Paul writes. He did not hold himself above the human in any of its dimensions. He did not lean on his divinity, however he would have understood that, to provide him with a way to make being human more fitting for a God. He did not exempt himself from needs or feelings or desires, or from the struggle and pain that often accompany them. He did not cling to the transcendent or leap into an over-spiritualized existence at the expense of his humanity. Rather, he emptied himself. And his self-emptying took two forms: profound *self-acceptance* and radical *self-disclosure*.

Kenosis As Self-Acceptance

Who was the self that Jesus of Nazareth accepted? What constituted his self-acceptance?

Jesus was a Jew. He was male. His origins were humble. He spoke Aramaic. He acquired a laborer's trade. He had a particular height, weight, body structure and physical appearance. He had a temperament, unique likes and dislikes, and clear, distinctive personality traits. He was born in Palestine during the Roman occupation, a fact that would have exposed him to political turmoil and religious upheaval from his youth. Like any other human being Jesus of Nazareth had strengths and weaknesses, gifts and limitations.

All of this defined the self that Jesus accepted. He lived within his Jewish heritage and his own male sexuality. He welcomed his social class, embraced the lifestyle of a carpenter's son, and entered fully into his own time in history. He accepted the boundaries of his human personality. He died when his time was up.

For Jesus, and for any human person, self-acceptance begins with the basics: the full acknowledgement of who we are personally, spiritually, physically, culturally, socially, educationally, intellectually, historically. But it does not stop there. Genuine self-acceptance is much more than a simple recognition of the obvious, or a static embrace of the present. It pushes us to take who we are on a journey. It urges us into the desert. It invites us to love ourselves so much that we will not let ourselves be less than we can be. Self-acceptance is the willingness to claim and to love who we are and the commitment to push that self-definition to its greatest possibility. It is just such a commitment that involves self-emptying.

When self-acceptance is so strong that it compels one to empty out anything that stands in the way of authentic personal growth, a dimension of true biblical kenosis is present. Paul's phrase from Philippians reminds Christians of just that fact.

Jesus accepted himself by emptying himself of all of the ways that human beings try to escape their flesh. He emptied himself of the excuses, the games, the tasks, the empty chatter and the superficial comments that people so often use to keep themselves safe. He emptied himself of flight into divinity when being human was uncomfortable. He emptied himself of the common temptation to hide his feelings, to seek self-protection and security in seclusion and isolation. He emptied himself of a compromising obedience toward the religious leaders with whom he had fundamental disagreements. He emptied himself of the practice of keeping rituals and laws that made strict religious observance more important than the needs and life experience of people. He emptied himself of all of the patriarchal, hierarchical ways of relating to

people so common in his day. He even emptied himself of the temptation to cling to God, to opt out of taking full responsibility for his own
life and choices.

Jesus did not empty himself for the sake of being empty. With every
act of self-emptying there was an embrace of something else that was
closer to the heart of the human. Each time Jesus of Nazareth said no to
skimming over the surface of his humanity, he said yes to accepting that
humanity in a way far deeper and with far more reverence than any
other human being had ever done. His self-acceptance reached into the
depth of his human identity, prompting him to welcome every sign and
experience of his humanness as both a gift and a responsibility.

His total acceptance of human emotion enabled him to grieve until
his bowels churned and to weep in the open. His acceptance of human
limitations brought him the experience of such bone-wearying fatigue
that even a storm-tossed boat did not rouse him from sleep. His acceptance of human interactions made him so present to people that every
sinew in his human flesh could feel the power spill out of his body when
he encountered another person in need. His acceptance of human hunger created an ache so powerful that he would search in the night for
the strengthening presence of God. His acceptance of his own truth, his
trust in his own vision, gave him strength to fight for both even in the
face of religious opposition.

The kenosis of Jesus was complete, so complete that there was space
enough for all expressions of his humanity to find fullness and integration.

Such complete self-emptying did not constitute self-diminishing behavior. To the contrary. Every temptation, every excuse that Jesus emptied out was a rejection of an obstacle toward fuller self-development,
self-development in the best Christian sense of the term. Such self-
development is not equated with self-aggrandizement or with egotistical
self-fulfillment, but with the actual development of the self, development that is at once whole and holy. It implies movement toward and
integration of the great commandment to love our neighbor as ourself.

To move more deeply into self-acceptance is to automatically move
more deeply into the experience of the genuine goodness of humanity,
our neighbor's humanity as well as our own. Self-emptying then becomes the gradual elimination of impediments to the deepest possible
experience of what is best in the human: potential for sharing, for giving
and receiving love, for lasting relationships, for the expression of creativ-

ity and generativity, for personal growth toward wholeness and holiness.

It is often said that love of neighbor is virtually impossible without simultaneous love of self. The dramatic examples of other-centered love seen in Jesus testify to a self-love and self-acceptance that must have been at the core of his life. He loved out of the fullness of his humanity, not out of its emptiness. He accepted others with such total compassion because he regarded his own humanity with such reverence.

The scriptures are full of exhortations to practice self-giving love. What the bible implies, and what psychology explicitly states, is that there has to be a reasonably well-defined self there in order for that self-giving love to have a starting place. Basic to the call to kenosis is the call to self-acceptance. Attempting to give a self that we have never come to know is like offering a gift to someone without knowing what is in the box, and without knowing whether it will hurt or help the other. Likewise, trying to offer a self to others that we have never come to accept is the same as giving something to another that we don't even like in the first place. Such an offer rarely feels like a gift to its recipient, and may even be resented. This is why many individuals with low self-acceptance levels meet repeated rejection when they try to give themselves to others in friendship. Lack of self-acceptance shows itself in subtle ways. Trying to hide it doesn't fool people. Smiling, acting happy on the surface, and doing things for others feels shallow without being rooted in basic self-acceptance.

Moving toward greater self-acceptance begins in the same way for us that it did for Jesus: consciously refusing to grasp at an easy way out of the human condition. It involves making a clear decision to enter flesh, to claim our heritage instead of blaming it or escaping it. It means being true to real feelings. It invites us to take a deep breath and plunge into the real work of shaping our possibilities and directing our energies toward bringing to reality the best definition we have of ourselves.

Kenosis As Self-Disclosure

If one dimension of the kenosis of Jesus involved self-acceptance, another involved self-disclosure. Jesus not only emptied out, he also emptied forth. He spilled out who he was to the other human beings with whom he shared flesh. He poured forth his words, his vision, his feelings, his ideas, holding nothing back. He opened up. He let others in. The full extent of his self-disclosure is expressed in John's gospel:

> I shall not call you servants any more,
> because a servant does not know
> his master's business;
> I call you friends,
> because I have made known to you
> everything I have learnt from my Father (Jn 15:15).

"Everything I have learnt from my Father." It is a phrase that can easily be over-spiritualized. We can imagine Jesus instructing the disciples in great theological truths, standing among them as the omniscient expert in heavenly matters. We can picture him handing down dogmas directly from God to all-absorbent followers. But is that a description of friendship? When one person passes on information unilaterally to others, does a bond of love develop, a bond so strong that it will transcend the violence of crucifixion and the permanence of death? When one person is the expert and the others are recipients of his or her wisdom, does interpersonal commitment grow to such an extent that lives are changed forever?

No. Friendship comes from sharing the heart, not sharing information. If the gospel writers remembered Jesus as one who developed bonds of lasting friendship with his followers, then we know that he related to them not as a resident expert but as a vulnerable companion.

Genuine friendship does not develop when there are real or perceived inequalities among people. It does not develop when one person controls the relationship. It does not develop when there is informational disclosure but no self-disclosure. If Jesus and his disciples actually grew to love one another, and to experience themselves as friends, then we know that Jesus revealed much more than abstract theological truths and cognitive ideas about the kingdom. We know that he revealed himself—his own raw humanity—to those who became his closest friends.

"Everything I have learnt from my Father." What was the "everything" that Jesus made known and how did he learn it? A major part of what Jesus made known during his lifetime did in fact concern those things he had come to believe about the kingdom of God. Jesus arrived at these convictions through a gradual process of reflection on the Hebrew scriptures, his own life experience, and prayer. It was a process that he believed had God as its source. Such a process would have involved struggle, search, frustration. It was all of this that constituted the "everything" that Jesus made known during his lifetime to his disciples and friends: the growing convictions, the moments of excitement, the feelings of discouragement, the questions, the insights, the breakthroughs. It was the communication of this "everything" that moved Jesus and his disciples from a master-slave relationship to one of friendship.

For Jesus, the difference between slavery and friendship was the difference between superficiality and intimacy. A slave is one who does not know the business of the other. A slave is kept in the dark. A slave has not experienced the kind of disclosure that makes known the deepest self of the other, and so cannot possibly be a friend. The best way to avoid friendship, then, is to avoid self-disclosure. Avoiding self-disclosure is also an effective way to oppress people. It keeps them slaves; it makes them captives of secrecy and victims of silence.

By contrast, a friend is one who does know the "everything" of the heart of the other. A friend is in the light. A friend is one who has listened to the ideas, shared the excitement, walked through the darkness, celebrated the joy, felt the pain, tasted the tears. A friend is one who has experienced the core of another and, in so doing, has come to know something of the real essence of the kingdom vision. It is the process of self-disclosure that turns acquaintances into friends, and followers into lovers.

Sometimes, with the stress on the element of mystery in religion, it is easy to identify Jesus of Nazareth simply as one more religious figure shrouded in mystery, a man too holy to know. We then forget how transparent he really was with his friends. Though they were often unable to fully understand, his attempts to disclose himself to them continued until his death.

The evangelists tell several stories of Jesus of Nazareth sharing his immediate inner experience with those closest to him. Their memories suggest that he has a style of self-disclosure supportive to the kind of deep friendship that he advocated:

> And taking with him Peter and the two sons of Zebedee,
> he began to be sorrowful and troubled. Then he said to
> them, "My soul is very sorrowful, even to death" (Mt 26:
> 37-38), (RSV).

The story in Matthew's gospel says that Jesus felt sorrowful and troubled. As soon as he became aware of these feelings, he shared them with his friends. It is an example of immediacy: revealing inner reactions as they are happening to those who have a right to know.

It is not an educational setting. There is no religious instruction to impart and no theological point to make. Jesus is simply alone with his friends. He is feeling sad and anxious. He wants them to know. He does not try to put up a messianic front or pay the I-have-to-be-strong-for-them role. Nor does he minimize his pain. It hurts "to death." He chooses openness over secrecy. Vulnerability over bravery.

It is only then that Jesus goes to pray. It is only after he had touched his truth and claimed his agony that he offers it to God. He does not rush to a private place to give his feelings to God until he has first given them to his friends. In the honesty of self-disclosure he finds the holiness of transcendence. Authentic prayer comes from deep within his own true state of being and feeling.

Self-Disclosure From the Viewpoint of Psychology

When John reminded Christians that Jesus was a person who developed lasting friendships by sharing "everything" with his closest followers, he stated a truth that psychologists would articulate much later from a different vantage point: Self-disclosure makes human intimacy possible.

When self-disclosure is defined psychologically, the focus shifts from Christianity to the principles of good mental health. Whatever the focus, the message is the same. Individuals need to develop an ability to make themselves known to others if they want friendship in their lives.

Letting people get to know us means more than letting them in on the facts about our life. It means letting them know the background fears that haunt our quiet moments, the heavy loneliness that sometimes lurks behind our smile, the passions that both excite and scare us. Self-disclosure means just what it says: disclosing the self. All parts of us. It means uncovering what we most want to hide, and telling what we most want to keep secret about ourselves to those who would be our friends.

Most specifically, self-disclosure means revealing our current reactions and feelings to those with whom we are relating. Without this information, others can only know our facade. A facade is not a building block for friendship.

Self-disclosure always implies verbal speech or some other form of communicating clear verbal messages such as sign language. We need to tell people what we want them to know about us and not leave them in the unfair position of having to decipher who we are by picking up oblique cues that we might send their way. The previous chapter on words and verbal clarity is particularly applicable here.

Self-disclosure can come in any tense. We can tell what we felt in the past, what stage of turmoil our life is in at the present time, or what we dream for the future. When we disclose what we are feeling and thinking right now, at the very moment of an interaction, psychologists often refer to the disclosure as "immediate." We are practicing the skill of immediacy in the sense that we are making known our current experience as it is happening. Being immediate with someone, particularly when we are revealing what we are feeling in relationship to the person with whom we are interacting, requires a high level of communication expertise. It presupposes that we are in touch with our most immediate feelings and able to name them as they are happening: "I feel very close to you right now . . . ." "What you just said gives me goose bumps. I feel so loved. . . ." "I'm having a hard time talking to you. I'm scared. . . ." "I'm starting to feel defensive . . . ." "I like it when you listen to me like this. It feels like you care."

A word that always needs to be attached to self-disclosure is *appropriate*. Just as extreme privacy or excessive guardedness is unhealthy, so is extreme disclosure. The individual who is in the habit of baring his or her soul to a stranger on a bus is likely desperate or ill. People who reveal the intimate details of their lives to casual acquaintances lack discretion. High-level self-disclosure during the first hour of interaction with a stranger may be appropriate in individual or group therapy, but it is generally not appropriate in other interpersonal situations. There is no such thing as instant intimacy. "Telling all" to a new acquaintance, or revealing very personal feelings too quickly usually causes healthy people to back away, and ruins whatever chance there might have been for the development of friendship.

Self-disclosure demands intense sensitivity and awareness if it is to be appropriate. The person who self-discloses effectively is able to sense how much to say, when to say it, where, and to whom.

The best test of the appropriateness of the level of self-disclosure is the friendship test: Does my life reflect the consistent presence of stable and close friendships that are mutually satisfying? Is there at least one person in my life who really knows my "everything," and who has shared his or her "everything" with me?

Self-Disclosure As Revelation

Creation involves divine self-disclosure. An aspect of the creative action of creatures is also to disclose, to make known what is deepest in ourselves to one another. One way of understanding this is to say that when we communicate we reveal God's image in ourselves. Another way of expressing this reality is to say that we reveal who God is when we reveal who we are to one another.

When we are able to share with one another our deepest truth, something of God is made known. When self-disclosure is taking place, revelation is taking place too. This means that all of our ideas, thoughts, feelings and behaviors have the potential to image God, to reveal the divine. That is not to say that all of these actions do, in fact, image God all of the time or even some of the time. What it does say is that to the extent that we are faithful to God's creative action in our lives, we reveal God when we share our truth with one another.

The early Christians saw God as the inspiration and source of all good thoughts and actions. When Paul encouraged the Corinthians to come to their assemblies with a revelation to share, he was not suggesting that some individual Christians had a direct pipeline to God from whom they received specific verbal messages (revelations) to be imparted to the others.

> At all your meetings, let everyone be ready with a psalm
> or a sermon or a revelation . . . but it must always be for
> the common good (1 Cor 14:26).

When Paul spoke of revelation, he was talking about self-disclosure in its most basic sense: making known the truth contacted in the holy places of a person's most authentic self. It was here that goodness dwelt, and here that God lived and spoke. A message spoken out of this truth was a message from God. The individual in touch with his or her authentic self was an individual in touch with God and was therefore able to reveal God in a way that the "out-of-touch" individual could not do.

How were the Christians to know the difference between self-disclosure and selfish disclosure? What would be the criteria for determining whether a disclosure had its source in God or in the self-interest of the individual? The ultimate test of honest revelation was its impact on the other Christians. If the revelation of an individual served the best interests of the community, if it was faithful to the essentials of inclusive love, then it was a revelation from God. Here the biblical truth and the

175

psychological reality converge: Both authentic revelation and appropriate self-disclosure come from truth and both promote relationships. For the Christian, the belief that truth has its source in God means that a person's own self-truth can reveal that God through self-disclosure. Certainly not all that God wishes to say will be said through human disclosure; God's revelation comes from many sources. But the individual who discloses the truth about himself or herself discloses something sacred—reveals the divine.

Revelation involves making known something that has previously been unclear. The term *revelation* usually implies some kind of divine action, the uncovering of something that is of more than human origin. Each time the word is used in the Christian writings, it emphasizes the importance of light over darkness, of things being manifest rather than hidden, or secrets being told and veils being taken away.

The message is striking. Divinity has to do with openness. It presses toward self-disclosure. Perhaps Jesus of Nazareth was most divine when he hung naked in the midst of the crowd, concealing nothing and hiding from no one. No one took his life from him. He laid it down of his own free will. In so doing, he laid it out for all to see. His self-disclosure was so complete that in the end he chose the radical nakedness of the cross over the safe concealment of his inner truth—and God's revelation.

Self-Emptying for the Sake of Service

We live in a world where biblical kenosis is too rarely practiced, where low self-worth often prevents people from genuine self-emptying. It is hard to let go when we are insecure. It is threatening to disclose our deepest self to another when that self is fragile or poorly defined.

The absence of kenosis is described by Paul when he said that Jesus did not cling (*harpagmos*) to his equality with God. *Harpagmos* literally means "robbery" or "rape." It alludes to more than innocent clinging. Robbery and rape are acts of violence. They hurt and even destroy people. *Harpagmos* involves the kind of clinging that is done at another's expense. It suggests taking something by force that belongs to someone else, grasping at something that robs others of what is rightfully theirs.

When applied to interpersonal situations, *harpagmos* describes all of those styles of clutching, hanging on and "taking" behaviors that do violence to relationships. Withholding words that rob others of forgiveness, clinging to our opinion, hanging on to the past, concealing feelings, hiding our real thoughts, using people by stealing their kindness and plundering their endurance—these are all subtle forms of psychological robbery. They take away other people's rights to reverent human sharing.

What, then, does Paul's choice of language suggest? What does it tell us about Jesus of Nazareth? And what are the implications for our time?

Paul's words give us a picture of a man who did more than avoid clinging to divinity. They describe a person who was unwilling to make others pay so that his life could be easier, a person who would claim no comfort for himself that would put a burden on the people in his life. His radical self-emptying was not centered in a concern over maintaining clean theological lines between the human and the divine. It was centered in a concern over maintaining honest connections with his friends, with people who had a right to share his center because they were involved in his life. He would not rob them of that right.

Clinging is easier than kenosis. It is easier to demand an apology than it is to spill out words of forgiveness. It is easier to cling to our opinions than it is to loosen our grip on them. It is easier to hold back our honest reactions in interpersonal situations than it is to empty them out for others to see, and perhaps to judge or reject.

Whenever we cannot release our hold on all of those things that we do to keep ourselves safe and comfortable, and whenever our holding on is costly to others against their will, then we are not practicing kenosis no matter how much we might be involved in a position of service or ministry. When our behavior causes others to pay the price of unnecessary anxiety, tension and fear, we are grasping at something that is not ours—the peace of mind that belongs to them.

The ultimate goal of kenosis is the welfare of people. True kenosis is therefore service-oriented. It serves relationships. It enables Christians to bond with one another. It calls them into a servant stance in behalf of one another.

> You were called, as you know, to liberty; but be careful, or this liberty will provide an opening for self-indulgence. Serve one another, rather, in works of love, since the whole of the Law is summarized in a single command: *Love your neighbor as yourself* (Gal 5:13-15).

For Paul, genuine service is always faithful to the Great Commandment. It is as loving toward self as it is toward neighbor. While there are many times when the mature Christian is called to serve others at his or her own expense, the overall picture of biblical servanthood is not hostile to nor consistently negligent toward self. It is loving. Loving, however, does not imply painlessness. Part of the very fabric of love is suffering. Moving toward greater levels of self-acceptance, an aspect of loving one-self, is demanding. Self-disclosure, as service offered in behalf of rela-tionships, can be agonizing.

In Matthew's gospel there is a story which refers to Jesus as the ser-vant willing to suffer in behalf of the people.

> That evening they brought him many who were possessed
> by devils. He cast out the spirits with a word and cured all
> who were sick. This was to fulfil the prophecy of Isaiah:
> *He took our sicknesses away and carried our diseases for*
> *us* (Mt 8:16-17).

He carried their dis-ease. He bore the burden of responsibility for their lack of comfort and walked with them toward wholeness. He did not shun the helpless or belittle the frail. He reached deep into his own wellness and offered them healing. His was the behavior of a servant, a suffering servant.

Jesus was willing to endure pain so others could live with less pain. He was willing to suffer gossip so a woman could experience acceptance. He was willing to suffer betrayal so Judas could have friendship. He was willing to suffer ultimate rejection, even rejection from his own religious tradition, so others could have his word.

Service costs. The servant suffers. There is the preoccupying agony of caring until it hurts. The sacrifice of time. The struggle to talk when every word aches. And no guarantees. Suffering servanthood is only for those who take following seriously. It is for those who can carry others because they have first carried themselves.

Throughout his earthly ministry, the proclamation of the kingdom of God was central to everything that Jesus did and said. There was both a present and a future dimension to the kingdom. It was at hand. It was now. It was flooding people's hearts and bursting into their lives in the most ordinary of ways every day. At the same time, it was not yet. It was to come. Jesus invited his followers to expect it, to prepare for it, to bring it about.

Whether Jesus spoke of the kingdom at hand or the kingdom to come, one thing was clear: The kingdom of God was a kingdom of love.

It was relational. It would be heralded not by mysterious signs or dramatic events but by lovers sharing their lives and friends staying faithful.

As followers of the Lover from Nazareth, friendship is our heritage. Building relationships is our call. Effective communication is foundational to that call. It prepares us to listen with our ears and to hear with our hearts. It fills us with longing to gather people in our arms as a hen would her chicks. It enables us to find a compassion powerful enough for outcasts and big enough for ourselves. It readies us to put down stones so we won't hurt even the sinners. It gives us words made flesh.

Notes

Introduction:

1. For a very thorough explanation of the contextual method of interpreting scripture, and a more detailed analysis of these questions, see the following:

   Daniel J. Harrington, S.J., *Interpreting the New Testament* (Wilmington, DE: Michael Glazier, Inc., 1980).

2. Ben Logan, *The Land Remembers* (New York, NY: Avon Books, 1975), p. 234.

Chapter 1: In the Beginning

3. Scholars do not agree on the exact rendering of the Hebrew *ruah elohim* or the Hebrew participle which follows it. *Ruah* can be translated as "spirit," "wind" or "breath." Some scholars believe that the phrase is best translated "the wind of God swept"; others prefer "God's Spirit hovered." The latter translation is consistent with images of the protective, watchful, hovering God found elsewhere in the Hebrew scriptures (Ex 19:4; Dt 32:11). For a commentary on this see the following:

   Bruce Vawter, *On Genesis* (Garden City, NY: Doubleday & Company, Inc., 1977), p. 41.

   Raymond Brown, Joseph Fitzmeyer and Roland Murphy, editors, *The Jerome Biblical Commentary* (Englewood Cliffs, NJ: Prentice-Hall, Inc., 1968), pp. 10-11.

4. The ideas of the Hebrew scriptures as the communication memories of the Israelites originated with Dr. Anna Polcino, SCMM, founder of the House of Affirmation, Whitinsville, Massachusetts.

Chapter 2: On That Day God Listened

5. Abraham Joshua Heschel, *The Sabbath* (New York, NY: Farrar, Straus and Giroux, 1978), pp. 22-24.

6. Robert Bolton, *People Skills* (Englewood Cliffs, NJ: Prentice-Hall, Inc., 1979), p. 32.

7. Ibid., p. 30.

8. Ibid.

9. Elizabeth Dodson Gray, *Patriarchy As a Conceptual Trap* (Wellesley, MA: Roundtable Press, 1982), p. 89.

Chapter 3: With a Sigh That Came Straight From the Heart

10. Reay Tannahill, *Sex in History* (New York, NY: Stein and Day Publishers, 1980), pp. 141-142.

11. Robert Plutchik, *Emotion: A Psychoevolutionary Synthesis* (New York, NY: Harper & Row, Publishers, 1980), pp. 128-151. Diagrams can be found on pages 157 and 164, respectively.

12. Ibid., p. 170. Numerous authors who have studied human emotion have compiled lists of various feeling words. Many such words can also be used to describe behavior. Using the word *boastful*, for example, I can *feel* boastful or I can *be* boastful. This list is presented to assist readers in expanding their feeling vocabulary.

13. Donald Senior, *Invitation to Matthew* (Garden City, NY: Image Books, 1977), pp. 67-70.

Chapter 4: Never Let the Sun Set on Your Anger

14. Plutchik, op. cit., p. 1.

15. Ibid., pp. 6-8.

16. Ibid., pp. 59-60.

Chapter 5: Zeal for Your House Will Devour Me

17. Kurt Hanks, *Motivating People* (Allen, TX: Argus Communications, 1982), pp. 59-60.

Chapter 6: Have Care for One Another

18. Gerard Egan, *The Skilled Helper* (Belmont, CA: Wadsworth, Inc., 1982), pp. 120-126.